ILA Study Guide V3

by Don OShall

The OFFICIAL Institutional Locksmiths Association Study Guide for Certification Testing

First Edition Written by Don OShall

This is a "work-for-hire" project so although author retains the right to use any and all material written by them in other productions or derivative works, primary copyright ownership will belong to the Institutional Locksmiths Association (INSTITUTIONAL LOCKSMITHS OF AMERICA).

ALL RIGHTS RESERVED

Note: The **LIST Council Dictionary** is included herein and portions are used throughout the book, in compliance with their official notice and are thus used by permission. The original document can be found at: http://www.thelockman.com/gloscopy.htm

The OFFICIAL Institutional Locksmiths
Association

Study Guide for Certification Testing

Locksmithing Education
Publishing

First Edition, ©
May, 2013 by
Donald OShall
Beverly Hills, FL -
USA

All rights
reserved.
No part of this book may be
reproduced in any form or by
any means, without permission
in writing from the publisher.

ISBN 978-1-937067-30-4

Library of Congress Cataloguing-in-Publication Data

OShall, Donald
 The OFFICIAL Institutional Locksmiths Association Study Guide for Certification Testing / by Don OShall

ISBN 978-1-937067-30-4
1. Industry-Security Measures-Management

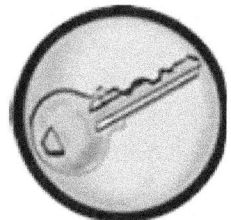

Locksmithing Education, LLC
12 South Lee Street
Beverly Hills, FL - 34465

TABLE OF CONTENTS

Basic Test Taking	1
1. **Overview and Introduction**	3
About the ILCP	4
2. **Architectural Builder's Hardware**	6
Architectural Finishes	7
Architectural Hardware Terms	8
Architectural Lock Functions	15
Functions without a deadbolt	15
Functions with a deadbolt	17
deadbolt only functions	18
3. **Basic Automotive Lock Terms**	**18**
Automotive Terms	20
4. **Code Books and Programs**	**21**
5. **Door Related Terms**	**22**
Handing Chart	24
6. **Door Closer Terminology**	**28**
Installation Types	29
7. **Exit Device Terminology**	**34**
8. **Master Key Basic Terms**	**37**
Levels of Keying	40
9. **Terms relating to Installation**	**44**
10. **Utility Lock Terms**	**52**
Disc or wafer tumbler	52
Flat Key Lever tumbler	53
General Utility Lock Terms	54
11. **Hazardous Warning Signs**	**57**
12. **Abbreviations and Acronyms**	**59**
Full List	60
Acronyms	**75**
Certification Acronyms	78
Master Keying Abbreviations	80
Life Safety Abbreviations	86
Abbreviations related to Doors	87
Abbreviations related to Keys	87
Abbreviations related to Pinning	89
Safe Work Abbreviations	91
Electronic Abbreviations	93
Utility Lock Abbreviations	95
Hinge related Abbreviations	95
Lock Type Abbreviations	95
13. **Electives for CJIL and CMIL**	**96**

ELECTIVE RESOURCES

13. Electives for CJIL and CMIL	96
E1 - The A2 SFIC	96
E2 - The A2 SFIC	96
E3 - The A2 SFIC	96
E4 - History	98
E5 - Fire and Life Safety Codes	99
E6 - Corbin Pinning	100
E7 - Medeco Product	101
E8 - BEST Product	102
E9 - Corbin-Russwin Product	103
E10 - Schlage Everest	104
E11 - KABA Peaks Classic	105
E12 - Basic Master Keying	106
E13 - Von Duprin	108
E14 - Rixson	108
E15 - Kwikset Pin Tumbler	109
E16- Schlage Primus	110
E17 - Schlage Cylinder	111
E18 - ASSA Twin V6000	112
XX - Forensic Locksmithing	113
XX- Electronic Access Control	114

COMMENT:

The ILA National Web Page at

http://www.institutionalLocksmiths.org

contains links to many additional resources, and will contain more as more benefits for members are added. Be sure to check there frequently.

Note that the links that changed may not be updated in your browser unless you click the refresh icon (usually a turning arrow) depending upon the browser settings on your computer. So it is a good plan to always hit the refresh icon whenever the information currency is vital or you are at a place which might have frequent improvements or changes. This applies to ANY website you visit.

Manufacturer's links may change beyond the capability of refreshing. Often they rename or relocate them. No one can do anything about that which is why the ILA struck arrangements for a free download whenever we could.

TABLE OF CONTENTS

Basic Test Taking	1
1. Overview and Introduction	3
About the ILCP	4
2. Architectural Builder's Hardware	6
Architectural Finishes	7
Architectural Hardware Terms	8
Architectural Lock Functions	15
Functions without a deadbolt	15
Functions with a deadbolt	17
deadbolt only functions	18
3. Basic Automotive Lock Terms	**18**
Automotive Terms	20
4. Code Books and Programs	21
5. Door Related Terms	22
Handing Chart	24
6. Door Closer Terminology	28
Installation Types	29
7. Exit Device Terminology	34
8. Master Key Basic Terms	37
Levels of Keying	40
9. Terms relating to Installation	**44**
10. Utility Lock Terms	**52**
Disc or wafer tumbler	52
Flat Key Lever tumbler	53
General Utility Lock Terms	54
11. Hazardous Warning Signs	57
12. Abbreviations and Acronyms	59
Full List	60
Acronyms	**75**
Certification Acronyms	78
Master Keying Abbreviations	80
Life Safety Abbreviations	86
Abbreviations related to Doors	87
Abbreviations related to Keys	87
Abbreviations related to Pinning	89
Safe Work Abbreviations	91
Electronic Abbreviations	93
Utility Lock Abbreviations	95
Hinge related Abbreviations	95
Lock Type Abbreviations	95
13. Electives for CJIL and CMIL	**96**

ELECTIVE RESOURCES

13. Electives for CJIL and CMIL	**96**
E1 - The A2 SFIC	96
E2 - The A2 SFIC	96
E3 - The A2 SFIC	96
E4 - History	98
E5 - Fire and Life Safety Codes	99
E6 - Corbin Pinning	100
E7 - Medeco Product	101
E8 - BEST Product	102
E9 - Corbin-Russwin Product	103
E10 - Schlage Everest	104
E11 - KABA Peaks Classic	105
E12 - Basic Master Keying	106
E13 - Von Duprin	108
E14 - Rixson	108
E15 - Kwikset Pin Tumbler	109
E16- Schlage Primus	110
E17 - Schlage Cylinder	111
E18 - ASSA Twin V6000	112
XX - Forensic Locksmithing	113
XX- Electronic Access Control	114

COMMENT:

The ILA National Web Page at

http://www.institutionalLocksmiths.org

contains links to many additional resources, and will contain more as more benefits for members are added. Be sure to check there frequently.

Note that the links that changed may not be updated in your browser unless you click the refresh icon (usually a turning arrow) depending upon the browser settings on your computer. So it is a good plan to always hit the refresh icon whenever the information currency is vital or you are at a place which might have frequent improvements or changes. This applies to ANY website you visit.

Manufacturer's links may change beyond the capability of refreshing. Often they rename or relocate them. No one can do anything about that which is why the ILA struck arrangements for a free download whenever we could.

Basic Test Taking

Although the purpose of this book is to help you prepare for a specific set of tests, there are some basic test taking skills that everyone should master before taking ANY test. Often these skills are the difference between a successful test and a failed one.

1. Get plenty of rest the night before. Easier said than done, right? But many people make the mistake of staying up late the night before the test "cramming". Rarely does this help. Instead, it raises the tension level on the day of the test and diminishes the test taker's ability to handle that stress.

2. Get a good, filling, nutritious meal on the day of the test. Make it high in fruits and vegetables with just a bit of protein. A heavy protein meal such as a triple order of bacon is likely to diminish your attention and sap your energy. Going without a meal or just drinking caffeine products such as coffee tends to raise the stress levels and take away from concentration. But don't overdo the size of the meal either. More, even fruits and vegetables, can be too much and sap your energy levels. So can high sugar breakfasts.

3. Most tests are either True and false or multiple choice. **If you know the correct answer to the question, answer it correctly. But if you don't, apply logic.**

4. If you have a true or false question and the **question contains an "all or nothing" statement** such as "all dogs are red" or "no dogs are red", the **likelihood is that the answer will be false**. True and False questions with the word "some" in them tend to be true more often than not. These are extensions of logic.

5. Similarly, if a question is multiple choice and possible **answers include all of the above or none of the above, it is likely to not be either of those, but more likely to be all than none**.

6. Of the remaining multiple choice answers, chances are that at least one is illogical and/or impossible or even downright silly. **Eliminating that obviously wrong answer** reduces the number of choices and increases your chance of getting the answer correct.

7. With the exception of a few specially designed tests that usually tell you they are the exception, an empty answer is a wrong answer. So in the case where you have no idea, at least choose one. **Don't leave it empty.**

If you are permitted scratch paper, write down the question number and come back to it unless test rules prevent it. When you have absolutely no clue, go for the middle answer of the possibly correct answers, and you have about a 1 in 3 chance of getting it right.

8. When you feel the stress, stop, take a deep breath and close your eyes. Visualize something pleasant for a second or two. Then go back to the test. Stress is the enemy. Don't let it defeat you.

9. Don't think too much. Tests are typically not intended to be confusing or misleading, so over-thinking a question often puts more into it than the test's author is likely to have intended.

10. Take the time to read and be certain of the question being asked. It is easy to see a familiar word and guess wrongly about what is going to be asked.

Some people learned these basics early and are "good test takers". Most people who think they don't test well simply never learned these Ten basic steps.

Section One: Overview and Introduction

The purpose of this book is twofold – first, to be a study guide to help prepare the locksmith to take the certification tests used in the Locksmithing industry, and in particular, the ILCP (Institutional Locksmiths Certification Program, began in 2003) and secondly, to be a resource for looking up terms that the locksmith may encounter in his or her daily work.

It is not a training manual. If you require education, there are several basic ways in which it can be obtained:

> Association Classes
> Books Correspondence
> Courses CDs, DVDs and
> Videotapes Distributor
> Classes Manufacturer
> Classes
> On-Line Courses

Most of these vary widely in when and where they are offered, so it is beyond the scope of this book to direct the reader to them, but books are more standardized in their availability. The most common sources are:

Locksmithing Education.com
http://www.Locksmithing Education.com/catalog.htm

The National Locksmith Bookstore
http://www.thenationallocksmith.com/

ALOA Bookstore
http://www.aloastore.com

Butterworth Publications
http://store.elsevier.com/searchResults.jsp?frPag=BS&FP=imprint&_requestid=1448041

DON'T FORGET TO CHECK YOUR LOCAL LOCKSMITH DISTRIBUTOR ALSO

We have tried to make this book fully redundant. That is, a term may appear in more than one area if it affects those areas.

The primary source for most of the material in this book is the LIST Council Dictionary, available at:
http://www.thelockman.com/gloscopy.htm

The LIST COUNCIL Dictionary is considered the security industry's overall official guide to terminology. However, this document is not limited to that group's endeavors. As Institutional Locksmiths, we often have needs for definitions beyond the scope of the average locksmith on the street, and as such, the terms that are common in Institutional Locksmithing may not be terms in common enough usage overall to reach the LIST Council's standards. Throughout this book we will try to indicate LIST preferred terms wherever possible, and an entire copy of the LIST Council Dictionary is a part of this book, by permission of the LIST Council.

An excellent example of what is meant by redundant use of terms occurs with the section on Abbreviations and Acronyms. Each term will be listed in an overall alphabetic listing of abbreviations and acronyms, along with a description of the typical usage area. Then there is a list of abbreviations and acronyms by usage area. Then, later in the book when the topic is that usage area, the list will be repeated. And finally, of course, all terms that appear in the LIST Council dictionary will also appear there.

This is not done to pad the thickness of the book. We want it to be as thin as possible to keep your costs down. But it needs to be done in order to make it as easy as possible for the reader to find what he or she needs.

After all, dear reader, this book is really all about YOU. Learn the terms, Use the terms, Share the terms. And above all, get Certified to show what you know.

About the ILCP

The Institutional Locksmith Certification Program (ILCP) is a series of exams that focuses on the unique character of institutional locksmithing.

The ILCP consists of three levels of certification;
Level 1 - Certified Institutional Locksmith (CIL)
Level 2 - Certified Journeyman Institutional Locksmith (CJIL)
Level 3 - Certified Master Institutional Locksmith (CMIL)

To earn the Certified Institutional Locksmith (CIL) designation the participant must pass a mandatory exam of approximately 250 questions that will measure a participant's knowledge of general of locksmithing.

Some of the subject areas include basic terminology, common lock and key parts, lockset functions and finishes, lock by-pass methods, use of code books or code programs for key fitting, hazardous warning signs, basic pinning and life safety codes. There are not any manufacturer "brand-specific" questions on the CIL exam.

To earn the Certified Journeyman Institutional Locksmith (CJIL) designation the participant must pass an "advanced" mandatory exam and elective exams that cover in-depth, manufacturer specific (e.g. Schlage, Corbin Russwin, Yale) subjects and institutional environment (e.g. university, hospital, detention) issues.

These exams reflect the security products and occupational circumstances that institutional locksmiths encounter daily.

To earn the Certified Master Institutional Locksmith (CMIL) designation the participant will have to pass additional elective exams not taken to earn the CJIL. The CJIL and the CMIL are advanced levels, and will also require the participant to have a specific amount of "years of experience" as an institutional locksmith.

This book is primarily intended to cover the mandatory portion of the exams. We will provide some basic guidance to where the reader might obtain more specific manufacturer information, but it will be incorrect.

Why would we publish something that we know is incorrect? We would not. But unfortunately, the internet is not like a book. A book can always be found if it is in print, and can usually be found moderately easily even if it is out of print. Web Pages, on the other hand, are -updated‖ frequently. The purpose of this is supposed to be to keep the information -fresh‖ and current.

Unfortunately, many IT department personnel or company web designers do not realize that actually using the pages means being able to remember where information is and go there when the information is needed. They frequently change web domain names and almost unbelievably often change which folders documents are in. But if they at least kept the document name the same, a person could theoretically search for that document. Unfortunately, even this is not the case. They often change the filename when they make updates, in order to avoid confusion on their part as to which is the old and which is the new. So the old simply disappears, making any published reference to it useless. And in the process, making the links we publish here wrong – at least some of them.

But the only alternative would be to provide a complete training course on each elective topic, and that is well beyond the scope of this book. That is why other books and courses exist.

While tests are constantly monitored for accuracy, the state of our industry is such that the products themselves even change frequently. For example, the test on Kaba Peaks had to be renamed Kaba Peaks Classic because Kaba Peaks came out with a new product line with differences that affect the accuracy of the answers. This is only one example.

We hope that in spite of this limitation, this book provides what you need.

Section Two: Architectural and Builder's Hardware

The terms -architectural‖ and -builder's‖ hardware are usually used interchangeably to describe the physical hardware that is applied to openings to control or protect them. This includes the locking hardware, but often when we hear the term it is meant to relate more to the non-locking hardware. For the purposes of this book, we will separate out terms relating specifically to locking or latching hardware, as well as terms relating to cabinet, desk and similar Utility hardware. We will also separate out terms related to door closers, which are primarily intended to automatically close a door. This chapter will focus on what remains. We will do so alphabetically, so that it is easier to research a term if needed.

The LIST Council describes architectural hardware as:

architectural hardware
n. 1. fittings applied to protect a surface of, or to facilitate use of movable members in a building such as doors, windows, or cabinets, 2. various fixtures used in building construction

For builders' hardware, it simply says to see the above definition of architectural hardware.

As you will recall from the Acronyms list, ANSI refers to the American National Standards Institute, which sets the guidelines for architectural hardware. Although many sections of their standard are important, several are more frequently referred to.

ANSI strike
n. any of many strikes designed to fit door and frame preparations as specified in the applicable document in the ANSI A115 series. Note: common usage usually refers to a strike with dimensions of 4 7/8" X 1 1/4", also sometimes called an -ASA strike‖.

ANSI 115.2
n. this series is the most commonly used type of strikes applied to commercial hardware. They are typically shaped more like a T than a D, whereas residential strikes often are closer in shape to a D. They typically range from 1 to 1-1/4 inches wide with an extended lip, and typically are either 2-3/4 inches or 4-7/8 inches in height.

ANSI 117.1
n. that section of the American National Standards Institute documents pertaining to handicap access

architectural finish code
n. one of a series of specification codes used to indicate the color and texture of a metal end product that can be installed. Some finish specifications also note the base metal characteristics and processes used to obtain the end product.

When we talk about the -Finish‖ in Locksmithing, we rarely are as specific as they get into when manufacturing products. We typically care only what it APPEARS to be, rather than how it is produced and what base material the apparent finish is applied to. There are literally hundreds of true finishes, but we concentrate on the US and BHMA (Builders Hardware Manufacturers Association) numbers that relate to common appearances.

Some manufacturers, such as Baldwin, have their own finish references that don't match exactly with any US or BHMA references because the base material is different. But these are rare.

Usually, an Institutional Locksmith need only be able to recognize a handful of apparent finishes, using either the US, BHMA or description in order to do everything they need to.

As an example, Corbin-Russwin and Schlage use the BHMA numbers, while Sargent and Yale use the US numbers. But all four recognize the descriptive terms.

The following chart, while by no means complete, covers just about every need the Institutional Locksmith is likely to have.

Description		BHMA	US	other
Bright brass,		605	US3	
Satin brass		606	US4	
Antique brass, blackened, satin, relieved		609	no US #	
Bright bronze		611	US9	
Satin bronze		612	US10	
Dark oxidized satin bronze, oil rubbed		613	US10B	
Satin nickel		619	US19	
Flat black coated		622	US22	
Bright chrome		625	US26	
Satin chrome		626	US26D	
Bright stainless steel		629	US32	
Satin stainless steel		630	US32D	
Sprayed Finishes	**BHMA**		**US**	**other**
Spray Primed	600			
Sprayed bronze	690			EB or EP or STAT
Sprayed black	693			ED
Sprayed aluminum	689			EN or SB
Sprayed Light bronze	691			BL
Duranodic, amber	694			
Duranodic, dark	695			

Builder's Hardware Terminology

astragal
n. a molding attached to the face of the active leaf of a pair of doors and overlapping the inactive leaf

An Astragal blocks the space between the doors in a pair of doors.

automatic flush bolt
n. a flush bolt designed to extend itself when both leaves of the pair of doors are in the closed position

A flush bolt is mortised into the top or bottom of the edge of the inactive door in a pair of doors where the inactive door is not controlled by an exit device. It secures the door. Manual flush bolts must be slid into the locked position by hand, while automatic flush bolts extend when the door reaches the closed position.

ball bearing hinge
n. a hinge which uses ball bearings between its knuckles to reduce friction
Hinges are medium duty pivots that permit a door to swing. The ball bearing hinge swings the door with less friction.

ball catch
n. a latch which uses spring pressure to force a ball bearing into a recess in its strike
Ball catches us a large ball bearing, which may vary in size depending on the size of the door they are intended to latch. Unlike a standard spring latch or dead latch used on locking devices, the ball catch does not have to be withdrawn to open the door. It simply requires sufficient pressure to overcome the spring pressure on the ball bearing.

barrel bolt
n. a surface mounted slide bolt which has a cylindrical shape

bullet catch
n. a friction catch with a projecting latch which is spherical or dome shaped
A bullet catch is similar to a ball catch, but slightly more resistant to being pulled open.

cane bolt
n. a surface mounted deadbolt designed to be moved by hand via a 90° bend in the bolt that serves as a handle

casement window
n. a window with a sash which pivots or swings to open
The swinging action separates it from a double hung widow which rises or falls vertically to open or close. Usually a casement window is operated by a rotating crank handle.

circular strike
n. a typically round, finished strike, usually driven into place in a drilled hole

This is similar to the cup bolt used in safes. Sometimes they are referred to as thimble strikes.

crane hinge
n. a three leaf hinge assembly with two of the leaves being mounted to the body and door and the third only to the other two leaves

cremone bolt
n. a surface mounted, top and bottom locking, deadbolt mechanism operated by a central handle

cup escutcheon
n. lock trim that creates a recess in a door face and does not protrude beyond the door face

cup handle
n. a fitting recessed into a door surface to provide a finger grip with which to move the door

cupboard latch
n. a latching mechanism typically surface mounted to the outside of cabinet doors or drawers

curved lip strike
n. a strike so shaped as to effect smoother function of the latch while the door is closing

cylinder collar
n. a plate or ring installed under the head of a cylinder to improve appearance and/or security

cylinder guard
n. a protective cylinder mounting device

Often a cylinder guard is similar to an oversize cylinder collar which is free spinning to reduce the possibility of applying torque to the cylinder itself.

door bumper
n. an obstruction installed to prevent a door or lock from contacting another object

This should NOT be confused with a door silencer, which is applied to the frame of the door to reduce noise when closing the door. The door bumper is applied to prevent problems when opening a door, not when closing it.

door holder
n. any device designed to maintain a door in the open position

door silencer
n. a bumper installed in the jamb stop to quiet the closing of a door

door viewer
n. a device with one or more lenses, mounted in a door at eye level, which allows a limited view through a door

drop ring
n. a looped handle which can pivot, typically recessed and falls flush with the door face when not in use

dummy cylinder
n. a non-functional facsimile of a rim or mortise cylinder used for appearance only, usually to conceal a cylinder hole

dummy trim
n. non-active trim applied for aesthetic purposes

dust box
n. an enclosure applied under a strike to enhance appearance and/or performance

dust cover
n. a device designed to prevent foreign matter from entering a mechanism through the keyway

dustproof cylinder
n. a cylinder designed to prevent foreign matter from entering either end of the keyway

dust proof strike
n. a typically floor mounted strike that has a spring loaded internal plunger designed to keep the receptacle free of dust and debris

Dutch door bolt
n. a bolt which secures the top section of a Dutch door to the bottom section

edge pull
n. a handle mounted on, or in, the edge of a sliding or pocket door for gripping to pull the door closed

elbow catch
n. an "L" shaped latching mechanism typically mounted to the inside of the inactive leaf of a pair of cabinet doors

escutcheon
n. a surface mounted trim which enhances the appearance and/or security of a lock installation

espagnolette
n. a top and bottom locking system with hooks at either end which rotate to draw a door or window fully closed

extended lip strike
n. a strike with a (usually curved) leading edge that protrudes to or beyond the edge of the jamb

extension flush bolt
n. a flush bolt that has a separate escutcheon and faceplate

filler plate
n. a usually flat piece of material used to; cover a hole or opening, provide a foundation for mounting additional hardware, or adjust the position of hardware as mounted

finish
n. a material, coloring and/or texturing specification
(see architectural finish)

flat goods
n. ancillary architectural hardware such as push plates, mop plates, stretcher plates, kick plates, etc.

flexible head mortise cylinder
n. an adjustable mortise cylinder which can be extended against spring pressure to a slightly longer length

flush cup pull
n. a flush pull with a circular cross-section

flush pull
n. a recess in a door or drawer which serves as a handle or grip

flush ring
n. a ring, recessed into a door, which swings out to serve as a handle

French doors
n. a set of double doors composed of many small glass panes and narrow stiles

friction catch
n. a door or cabinet latching device which contains no actuator and is released by applying a measure of force in the opening direction

Ball catches and bullet catches are examples of this type of device.

full lip strike
n. a strike plate for a latch with the lip extending the full height of the strike

full mortise hinge
n. a type of hinge designed for mortising into the edge of the door and into the rabbet of a door frame

gravity pivot hinge
n. a hinge with complimentary sloped or V shaped knuckles on each leaf that cause gravity to turn the door back to the closed position

grip
n. the knob, lever, thumbpiece, push-pull operator, etc. of any working trim

half-mortise hinge
n. a hinge which has one leaf mortised into the door and the second leaf applied to the surface of the frame

half-surface hinge
n. a hinge which has one leaf mounted onto a face of the door and the second leaf mortised into the frame

hook bolt
n. a lock bolt shaped in the general outline of a hook. Normally used on sliding doors or where spreading of the frame and door is a possible attack.

keyhole plate
n. an escutcheon for a keyhole

kick plate
n. a protective plate mounted on the bottom of a door to prevent damage to minimize damage to the door

knuckle
n. the part of a hinge that is formed to accept a hinge pin and act as a pivot surface for another knuckle

latch guard
n. a plate or combination of interlocking pieces designed to block access to the edge of a latch when the door is shut

latching threshold
n. one which has a shape designed to act as a strike
(The threshold is the plate at the bottom of many door openings.)

lip (of a strike)
n. the extended (usually curved) leading edge of a strike

lite
n. a hole in a door or wall to admit light, usually with glass or another transparent or translucent pane

mop plate
n. A narrow plate fixed to the bottom of a door for protection against soiling from a mop; similar to a kickplate

mullion
n. a vertical center post in the frame of a pair of doors

multi-color finish
adj. of or pertaining to a lockset whose finish is different for different trim components on one side of a door

muntin
n. a structural member in a door or window used to divide a large lite into smaller ones

peep hole
n. a small lens or opening which allows a limited view through a door
(also called door viewer)

pitcher handle
n. lock trim which serves as a pull and is generally perpendicular to the door at its top mount, then bends and tapers to its bottom mount

pivot
n. a hinge with a fixed pin and knuckle, forming a single joint

pocket strike
n. an electric strike which does not require a face cut in the door jam, yet allows operation of the boltwork of the door lock, often by manipulating the locking and deadlatching portions via end pressure

pull handle
n. trim for gripping to apply pulling force to a door

pull plate
n. a generally flat and commonly rectangular trim with an attached handle for pulling open a door

Pullman keeper
n. a type of keeper which is shaped to operate with the radiused contour of a Pullman latch

Pullman latch
n. a type of latch which pivots like a hinge and whose locking side is radiused

push plate
n. a generally flat and commonly rectangular trim mounted for hand contact to push open a door

sash lock
n. a type of window lock
(commonly used on double hung windows)

scalp
n. a thin piece of metal which is usually crimped or spun onto the front of a cylinder. It determines the cylinder's finish and may also serve as the plug retainer.

sex bolt
n. a nut and bolt set used to through bolt, with a closed nut basically flush with the mounting surface creating the appearance of a carriage bolt

split astragal
n. an astragal constructed of two pieces; each piece being mounted on either door of the pair, and abutting to create a seal

split finish
adj. of or pertaining to a lockset whose finish is different on each side of the door

spring hinge
n. a hinge incorporating a mechanism to apply automatic closing force

surface pull
n. a handle or grip attached to the surface of a door or drawer

swing clear hinge
n. a hinge that allows the door to swing far enough away from the jamb to fully clear the opening at 90 degrees open

T-strike
n. a strike whose lip spans the middle portion (but not the full height) of the strike

template hinge
n. a hinge with dimensions, hole locations and tolerances which conform to ANSI standard A156.7

thumb turn
n. a actuator which can be turned by thumb and forefinger

thumb turn cylinder
n. a cylinder with a turn knob rather than a keyway and tumbler mechanism

thumbpiece
n. a generally flat, projecting latch actuator found above a grip handle and depressed by the thumb

Architectural Lockset Functions

Lockset Functions Without a Deadbolt

Classroom - The latchbolt is retracted by the grip on either side unless the outside grip is locked by the outside key.

Classroom Security - The latchbolt is retracted by the grip on either side unless the outside grip is locked by either the inside key or the outside key. Operating the inside grip always retracts the latchbolt.

It is probably worth noting that Classroom Security locksets may utilize an electronic token or similar device rather than a traditional key and still are considered Classroom Security function.

These have also been referred to as Crisis Response Management function or CRM.

ENTRY FUNCTION: This lock has a key on one side and a push button on the other. When the button is depressed, it can only be unlocked from the outside with a key. Turning the handle on the inside will make the button pop out which unlocks the door until either the button is depressed again or it is locked from the outside with a key. This is mostly used on doors that require some type of security such as exterior and office doors.

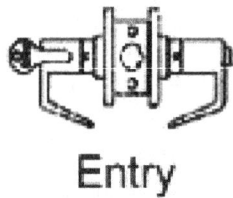

Entry

Institutional (Asylum) - The latchbolt is retracted by a key on either side. The grips on both sides are rigid.

Office - The latchbolt is retracted by the grip on either side unless the outside grip is locked by the toggle or outside key. Operating the inside grip does not unlock the outside grip.

Passage - The latchbolt is always retracted by the grip on either side. Both grips are always free. This has no key or push button on either side. It consists of two blank handles. Both sides are always unlocked. This is sometimes used on stairwell doors or any other doors where all you require is to have the door latch behind you but not lock so that it can be opened at all times.

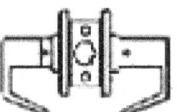

Passage

Privacy - The latchbolt is retracted by the grip on either side unless the outside grip is locked by the inside thumb-turn, button, or key. Operating the inside grip unlocks the outside grip. An emergency release tool unlocks the outside grip.
Some manufacturers offer models that also unlock the outside grip when the door is closed (i.e. the door can only be locked from the inside if the door is fully closed - locking an open door then closing the door unlocks the outside grip). This lock has a push button on one side and an emergency release on the other side. It is made so that it can be locked from the inside but can be opened from the outside with a tool (usually a coin or screwdriver will do) in case of an emergency. This is mostly used on bathrooms.

Privacy

Public Restroom - The latchbolt is retracted by the inside grip or an outside key. The latchbolt is retracted by the outside grip unless the grip is locked by a key from the inside. The latchbolt / outside grip cannot be locked by a key from the outside.

Storeroom - The latchbolt is retracted by the inside grip or outside key. The outside grip is optional, but when provided it is always rigid. This lock has a key on one side and a blank handle on the other side (no key or button). It remains locked all the time from the outside (key side) and requires the key to open it every time you open the door. It is always unlocked from the inside. This is mostly used on storage and utility rooms or a janitor's closet.

Storeroom

Lockset Functions With a Deadbolt

Apartment - The deadbolt is engaged or retracted by an outside key or an inside thumb-turn. When the deadbolt is engaged the outside grip is locked and will not retract the latchbolt. When the deadbolt is engaged the inside grip simultaneously retracts both the deadbolt and the latchbolt. The latchbolt alone can be locked by a toggle (engaging the deadbolt is not required to lock the outside grip).

Classroom Security - The deadbolt is engaged or retracted by key on either side. When the deadbolt is engaged the outside grip is locked and will not retract the latchbolt. When the deadbolt is engaged the inside grip simultaneously retracts both the deadbolt and the latchbolt and leaves the outside grip unlocked.

Dormitory - The deadbolt is engaged or retracted by an outside key or an inside thumb-turn. When the deadbolt is engaged the outside grip is locked and will not retract the latchbolt. The latchbolt is retracted by the grip on either side as long as the deadbolt is retracted. When the deadbolt is engaged the inside grip simultaneously retracts both the deadbolt and the latch.

Storeroom - The latchbolt is retracted by the grip on either side. The deadbolt is engaged or retracted by the outside key or the inside key / thumb-turn. The latch and deadbolt operate independently.

Store Door - The latchbolt is retracted by the grip on either side. The deadbolt is engaged or retracted by the key on either side. The latch and deadbolt operate independently.

Deadbolt Only Functions

Deadlock - The deadbolt is engaged and retracted by an outside key. An optional inside key or thumb-turn will engage or retract deadbolt.

Classroom Deadlock - The deadbolt is engaged and retracted by an outside key. An inside thumb-turn will retract the deadbolt only (it will not engage the deadbolt). An optional inside key will engage the deadbolt.

Section Three: Car Lock Basics

Institutional Locksmiths don't usually have a lot to do with automotive lock servicing, but they should still be aware of some basics for those times when someone important to the institution has a problem.

The following are some basics on service and terminology related to the topic.

Most cars in the 1940's and some into the 1960"s were opened by a vent window bypass (which was why vent windows were discontinued by auto manufacturers); most cars in the 1950's to 1970's were opened with a flat tool generally called a "Slim Jim" (after one brand of such tool); most of the vehicles from the 1980's and 1990's were opened by one of three tools, an F rod, a J rod or a U rod; and most of the vehicles since then are opened by wedging the vehicle window and inserting an extra-long tool (not unlike a straightened super giant coat hanger in appearance) with either a hook or loop on its end to activate the inside button or handle.

The vent window opener typically was two parts-one to depress the button, releasing the handle on the vent window, and one to rotate the handle itself. The -Slim JimII and similar tools were flat steel with a notch to catch either the vertical linkage or the movable pawl on the back of the lock, which acted as a tailpiece and rod actuator. The F and J rod tools linked the horizontal or vertical linage moving the inside lock/unlock button. The U tool slipped under the glass and came back up under the inside lock button, catching its lip. And the long reach tools are inserted between the window and frame to the interior of the car to operate the inside handle or lock/unlock button,

Fitting a key to cars typically involved either reading disc (wafer) locks or impressioning locks or disassembling and decoding them. With the advent of the transponder and computers (beginning in 1992 on some models) the trade changed its methods, Sometimes keys are now made by subscribing to a source which matches VIN numbers to key cuts, while other vehicles require interrogating the on-board computer using special, very expensive equipment.

The use of laser cut (or double-cut) keys or keys with a track cut on the side, which started on high end imported vehicles, Is rapidly spreading and has further complicated key cutting for some modern vehicles.

Terms you should know:

accessory position
n. the position of an ignition switch intended to permit the use of radio or other equipment without turning on a drive train component

chip key
see 'transponder key', 'VATS key' or 'PATS Key'

garage door lock
n. a rim lock mechanism designed for use on an overhead door, which mechanism has a spring loaded bolt which automatically locks the door's bolt mechanism

ignition key release
n. a button or other actuator which must be pushed before a vehicle's ignition key may be turned to the withdrawal position

ignition lock
n. the lock assembly associated with a vehicle's engine on-off switch and starter

ignition puller
n. a tool for removing an ignition cylinder by pulling outward on it

impression
n. 1. the mark made by a tumbler on its key cut 2. v. to fit a key by the impression technique

impression technique
n. a means of fitting a key directly to a locked cylinder by manipulating a blank in the keyway and cutting the blank where the tumblers have made marks

impressioning tool
n. 1. a tool designed to hold a key blank while making a key by the impression method, 2. a tool which fits into a keyway and holds a material that accepts impression marks easily

laser cut
adj. 1. a way of cutting a key so that the roots of adjacent cuts are connected by a straight-line cut; 2. a way of cutting a key so that the root of a shallow cut is widened until it intersects the included angle of an adjacent deeper cut

linkage
n. 1. any of various parts in a lock that help transfer motion to the bolt of a lock from a cylinder, turnpiece or other actuator not mounted to or touching the bolt/lock case, 2. part of the interconnected boltworks of an automotive lock

PATS
abb. Passive Anti-Theft System

pawl
n. the cam of certain automotive cylinders

primary key
n. the key which operates the ignition and/or ignition and doors depending on year of manufacture.

progression chart
n. a list of combinations to consider when fitting keys to a lock with only a partial bitting known, typically arranged to minimize the number of key blanks needed

secondary key
n. the key which operates the trunk or hatch and possibly also the doors, depending on year and make of vehicle.

trim panel
n. the decorative and functional assembly, which covers the inside surface of a vehicle, door

try-out key
n. a manipulation key which is usually part of a set, used for a specific series, keyway, and/or brand of lock

VATS
abb. Vehicle Anti-Theft System

VATS interrogator
n. a device which determines the resistor value required to complete the ignition circuit. It also reads the value of the resistor in a VATS key.

VATS key
n. a key for some General Motors vehicles which contains a resistor chip that must be qualified by the vehicle in order to run

Vehicle Anti-Theft System
n. an electronic system in some General Motors vehicles which uses a resistor pellet of varying value imbedded in a mechanical ignition key

Section Four: Code Books and Code Software for Key Fitting

There is nothing magic or difficult about these items. They are basically like any other type of catalog or catalog software. You use what you know to find what you need to know,

You might know the series, the lock manufacturer, the actual key cuts, what type of device it is used on or just one code number. From that you hope to get to all the other items on that list. You go to the table of contents, index or appendix, find the category you now and try to find the page on which it might appear and give you the rest of the available information. Sometimes there will be more than one answer and you will need to sort through the possibilities till you determine the correct one, Occasionally instead of giving an answer directly, it may give an alternative answer, such as a different code series but with the same answers. You might want OM1 to OM400 and it may direct you to instead use DE1 to DE400. Or, it may be derivative. OM series 1 to 400 may equal DE300 to 600 minus 200, in which case OM400 = DE600.

Some codes are not published or have yet to be decoded. Some never will. Others may instead be some form of encryption.

The simplest form of encryption is a Direct Code. In a Direct Code, a letter or number or symbol often is a part of the code and designates the keyway or lock series, and the rest of the code is the bitting (combination of cuts on the key).

The next simplest is a substitution code, where one letter or number is substituted for another.

Beyond that, there are ciphers, monofeds, bifeds, arrays, tables, and algorithms. There are also true blind codes, where a code is simply assigned to a bitting. These are what most code books concentrate on.

Chapter five: Terms Related to Doors

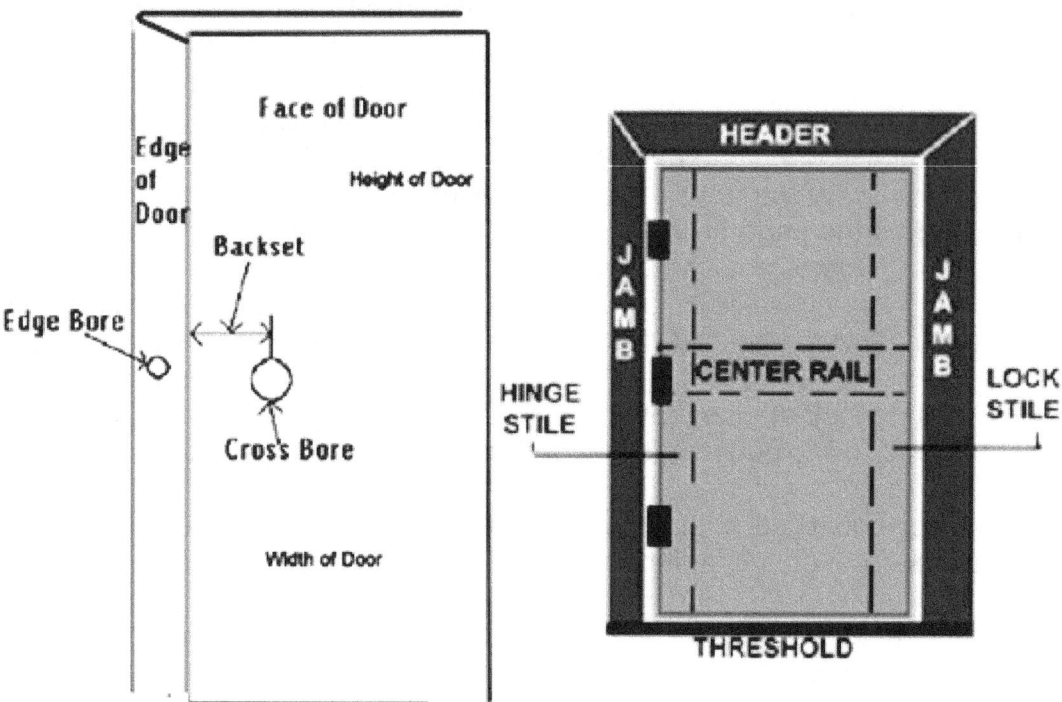

astragal
n. a molding attached to the face of the active leaf of a pair of doors and overlapping the inactive leaf

HINT: An astragal is attached to one door in a pair of doors; a mullion is a post between them.

backset
n. the distance between the center of a cross-bore and the bolt edge of a door or drawer

bevel (of a door)
n. the pitch on the leading edge of a door which allows clearance for closing

bi-fold door
n. a door with two or more sets of hinges, the additional set(s) allows the door to have an accordion action when opened

C label
n. a classification by Underwriters Laboratories for doors with 3/4 hour rated fire protection

Center Rail
n. the center portion of the door where an -exit deviceǁ(sometimes called a -crash barǁ by consumers) is typically mounted.

coordinator
n. in conjunction with a pair of doors, a device designed to cause the inactive leaf to close first

cross-bore
n. a hole drilled into the face of a door where a bored or interconnected lockset is to be installed

door control
n. any device which controls the opening, closing or position of a door

door holder
n. any device designed to maintain a door in the open position

door silencer
n. a bumper installed in the jamb stop to quiet the closing of a door

door swing
adj. the direction and degree to which a door opens, as LH 90°, RH 180°, etc.

door viewer
n. a device with one or more lenses, mounted in a door at eye level, which allows a limited view through a door

double- acting door
adj. a door that may be pushed open from either side

drive-in
adj. pertaining to a latch or bolt with a round face

edge-bore
n. a hole drilled into the edge of a door where a bored or interconnected lockset is to be installed

effective throw
n. the distance a deadlatch remains projected when the guard bolt has been engaged and end pressure is applied to the latch

filler plate
n. a usually flat piece of material used to; cover a hole or opening, provide a foundation for mounting additional hardware, or adjust the position of hardware as mounted

handed
adj. pertaining to hardware which is manufactured only for application on doors with a specific orientation

Recognizing the Door Hand
(Also called "Swing" by customers)

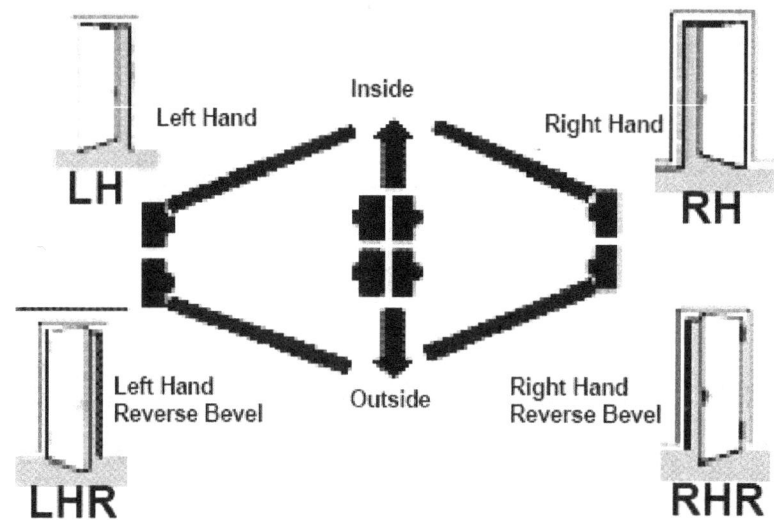

Note: When purchasing doors from a retail location be aware that many box stores do not use proper terminology. A -Right Hand Outswing‖ in these retailers is actually a Left Hand Reverse, and a -Left Hand Outswing‖ is actually a Right Hand Reverse.

header
n. the horizontal, top, member of a door jamb
(also known as Top Jamb)

Hinge Stile - The edge of the door where a hinge or hinges of some sort is intended to be put to hang the door.

hollow core door
n. a non-metal door with structural reinforcement creating air pockets between the two faces

hollow metal door
n. typically a door made of sheet metal on all surfaces and lightly reinforced to make it rigid

jamb
n. the vertical components of a door frame

Kalamein door
n. a metal clad door that has a wood filler

lock stile
n. the vertical edge of a door designed for lock or latch installation

mop plate
n. A narrow plate fixed to the bottom of a door for protection against soiling from a mop; similar to a kickplate

mullion
n. a vertical center post in the frame of a pair of doors

muntin
n. a structural member in a door or window used to divide a large lite into smaller ones

narrow stile
adj. pertaining to aluminum doors with stiles generally between 1-3/4 and 2-3/4 inches wide

overhead stop
n. a door stop which contacts the door near the top

peep hole
n. a small lens or opening which allows a limited view through a door

pocket door
n. a door which opens by sliding into a hollow wall

pocket strike
n. an electric strike which does not require a face cut in the door jam, yet allows operation of the boltwork of the door lock, often by manipulating the locking and deadlatching portions via end pressure

positive latching
n. the condition of a door being secured such that manual operation of the latch or bolt mechanism must occur before it may be opened

prep
n. 1. the location and dimensions of the cut out(s) and reinforcing in a door or frame required to accept a piece of hardware. 2. v. to prepare a door or frame for installation of a lock or other hardware

pull handle
n. trim for gripping to apply pulling force to a door

pull plate
n. a generally flat and commonly rectangular trim with an attached handle for pulling open a door

push plate
n. a generally flat and commonly rectangular trim mounted for hand contact to push open a door

rabbeted door
n. a door having and edge contoured with an offset creating two surfaces which form an overlap at the abutting edge

rail
n. the horizontal construction member located on the top and bottom of a door

reveal
n. the distance measured from the trim surface of the jamb to the leading face of the door on the stop side when closed

reverse bevel
adj. pertaining to the bevel of a door which swings towards the outside

reverse strike
n. a strike used for rim mounted hardware used on reverse bevel doors

reversible
adj. pertaining to hardware that is manufactured in a way, which allows field assembly or adjustment to accommodate installation on doors with different orientations

right hand (man door)
adj. pertaining to an inward swinging door with hinges on the right side, using the outside of the door as reference

right hand reverse bevel (door)
adj. pertaining to a right handed door which swings outward

single acting (door)
n. a door which swings from the latched position in only one direction

split astragal
n. an astragal constructed of two pieces; each piece being mounted on either door of the pair, and abutting to create a seal

spring hinge
n. a hinge incorporating a mechanism to apply automatic closing force

stile
n. the vertical construction member located on either edge of a door

stop (of a door)
n. the projecting portion of a doorframe upon which the door rests when closed

Threshold – the saddle beneath the door. Often this has a lip with weather stripping of some sort.

Top Rail – The top portion of the door where a surface applied door closer most commonly is mounted.

Warnock Hersey
n. an independent testing laboratory capable of field rating fire doors

wide stile
adj. pertaining to aluminum and hollow metal or wood doors with stiles 5 inches wide or larger

Section Six: Door Closer Terminology

backcheck
n. the resistance provided by a door closer as a door is opened

closer size
adj. a numerical value related to the applied force of a door closer, with a larger number being a stronger force. Older closers were assigned alphabetic size designations, where A was the smallest.

corner bracket
n. a door closer mounting plate attached to the upper corner of the jamb

delayed action closer
n. one which has a specific hold-open interval before it moves a door toward the latching position

door closer
n. a device designed to regulate the closing of a door automatically by various means

door control
n. any device which controls the opening, closing or position of a door

door swing
adj. the direction and degree to which a door opens, as LH 90°, RH 180°, etc.

double-acting closer
n. a door closer designed to be used on a double-acting door

double- acting door
adj. a door that may be pushed open from either side

floor closer
n. a door closer installed below the door at the floor surface, generally also acting as a bottom pivot for the door

hold open
n. 1. a function of self-latching hardware which allows a lock to be set in a non-latching mode 2. A function of a door closer, or separate hardware device, which allows the door to be retained in an open position

hold open arm
n. a door closer arm with the capability of maintaining the door in the open position

latching speed (of a door closer)
n. the final speed of a door just prior to closing

non-sized closer
n. a door closer with infinitely adjustable closing force between specific sizes

parallel arm
n. a type of door closer and/or closer mounting which leaves the arm generally parallel to the door face when closed

self-closing
adj. pertaining to doors or covers which have a continuous force applied in the closing direction

sex bolt
n. a nut and bolt set used to through bolt, with a closed nut basically flush with the mounting surface creating the appearance of a carriage bolt

shoe
n. 1. a bracket which attaches the arm of a door closer to the door or frame 2. the surface mounted case and guide components of an exit device 3. a mortise lock component which transfers pivoting motion of a thumbpiece to linear movement of the latch bolt

sweep speed
n. the speed at which a closer moves a door from open to the point where latching speed is engaged

top jamb mount
n. surface application of a door closer body directly to the header

There are many ways to mount a door closer.

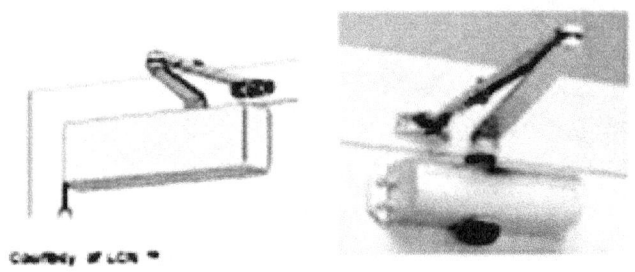

REGULAR ARM
(Inside of inswinging door
or outside of outswinging door)

There are many ways to mount a door closer.

 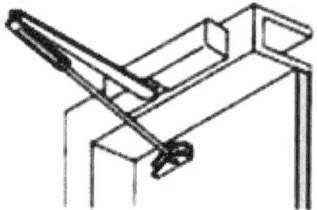

Courtesy of Corbin Russwin

TOP JAMB MOUNT
(inside of outswinging door)

There are many ways to mount a door closer.

TOP Jamb Mount with a Drop Down Bracket

(Inside of outswinging door)

There are many ways to mount a door closer.

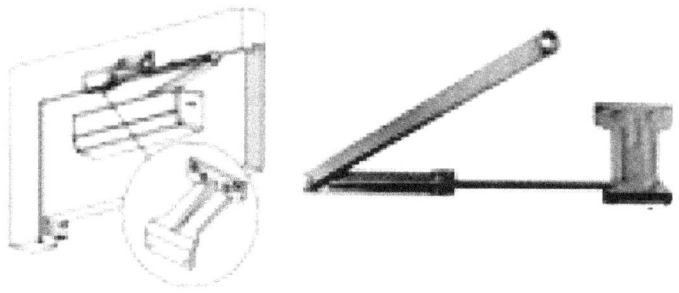

Parallel Arm Mount with a Parallel Arm BRACKET

There are many ways to mount a door closer.

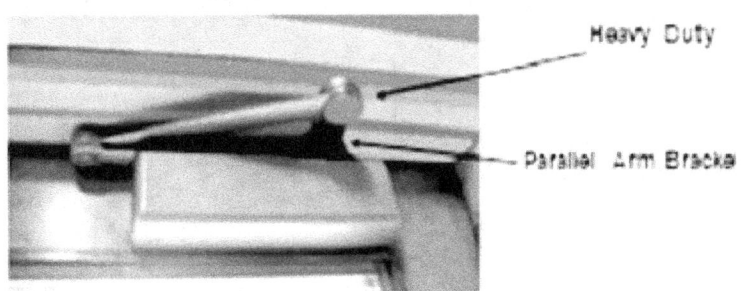

**PARALLEL ARM MOUNT WITH A
HEAVY DUTY PARALLEL ARM BRACKET**

(inside of outswinging door that might take a lot of usage)

There are many ways to mount a door closer.

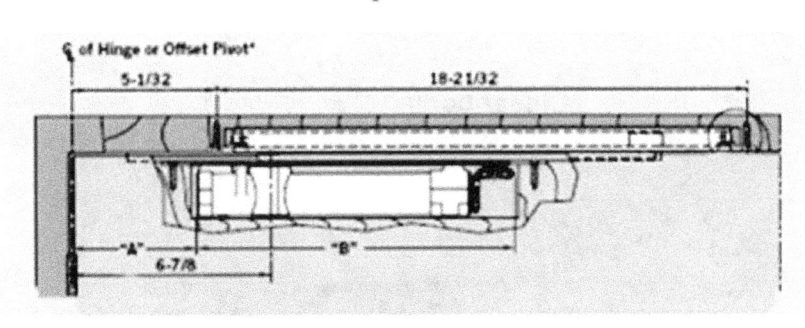

Courtesy of Dorma ™

CONCEALED IN TOP RAIL
(mortise installation - requires
specially prepared doors)

There are many ways to mount a door closer.

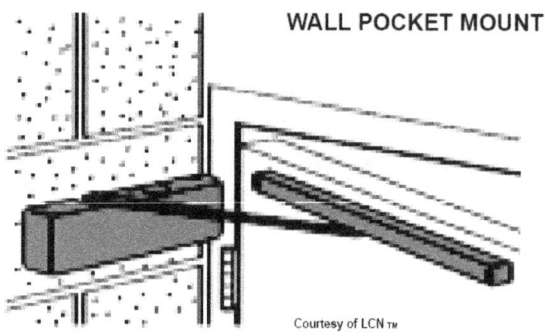

Wall Pocket Mount with Door Holder Track

There are many ways to mount a door closer.

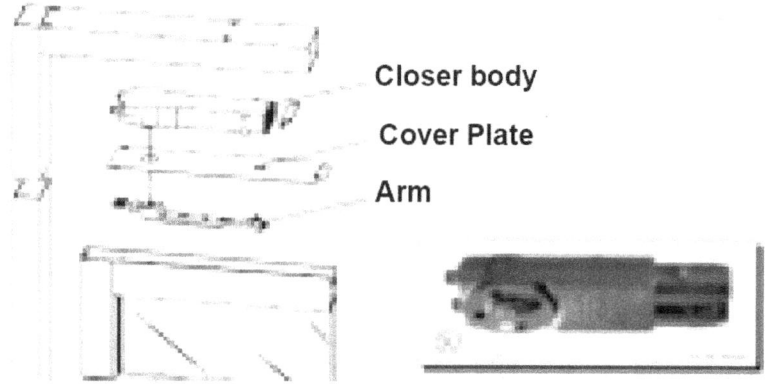

CONCEALED IN HEADER

There are many ways to mount a door closer.

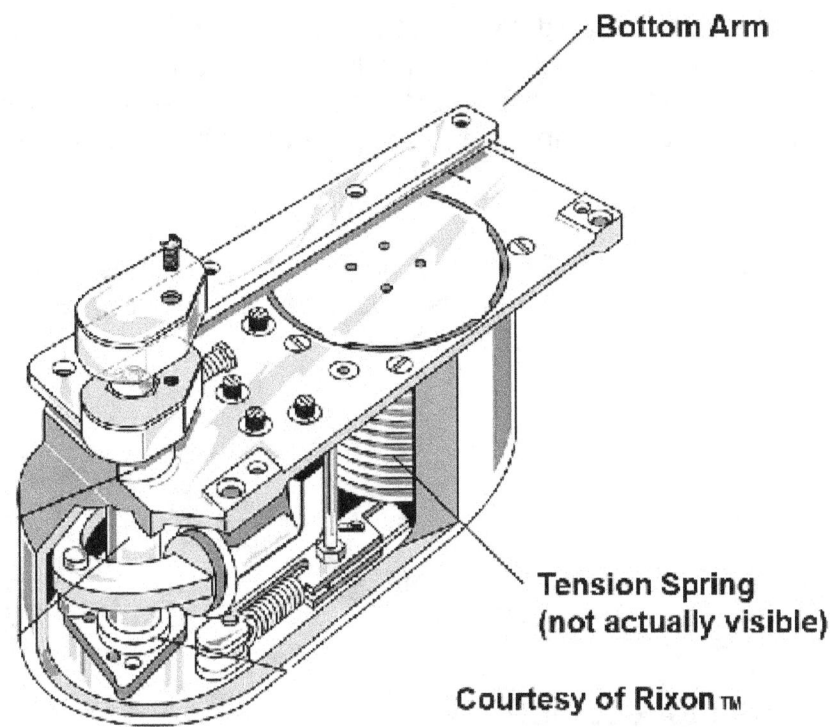

Courtesy of Rixon™

CONCEALED IN FLOOR
(INSTALLED IN SPECIAL POCKET BELOW DOOR)

Section Seven: Exit Device Terms

Exit devices are locks designed to permit people to exit an area quickly and easily. After a major fire in the early 1900's, a gentleman named Prinzler invented a locking device that used a pivoting bar to actuate the latch retraction, as shown here. He named his company Von Duprin, and today they are still a major manufacturer in the market for exit devices.

To begin with, exit devices are divided into cross-bar and pushpad (also sometimes called touchpad) types. The pushpad sits flat on the door typically, while the crossbar device is raised off the door by two lever arms.

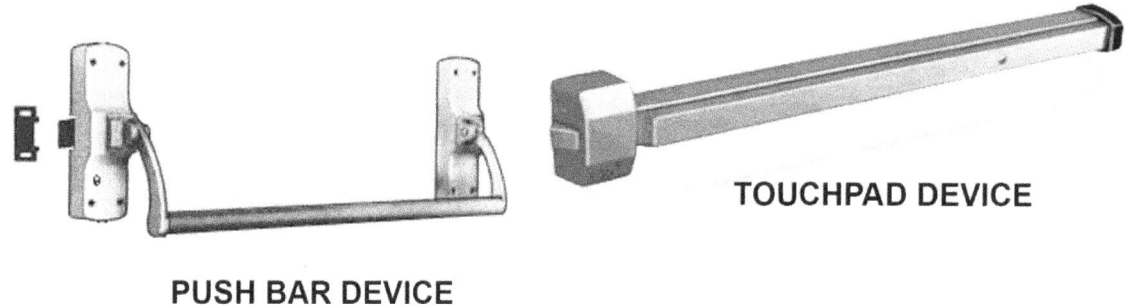

PUSH BAR DEVICE   **TOUCHPAD DEVICE**

Next we have the mounting method: Rim (or surface), Mortise or Vertical Rod (which can be visibly mounted on the surface or concealed (hidden inside a channel in the door).

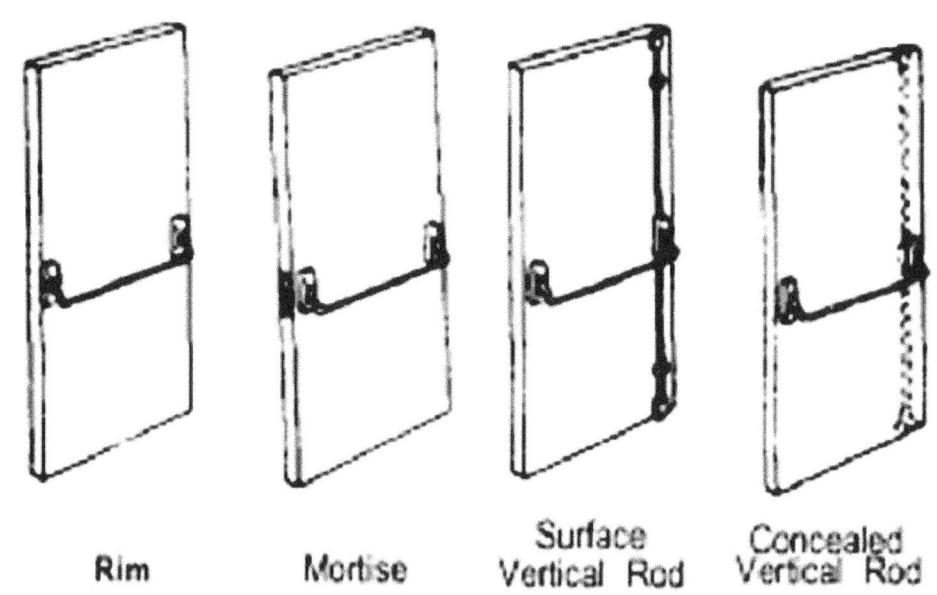

Rim   Mortise   Surface Vertical Rod   Concealed Vertical Rod

Some devices are top rod only or like the Sargent shown here are top and center latching. These resist problems commonly associated with a bottom rod.

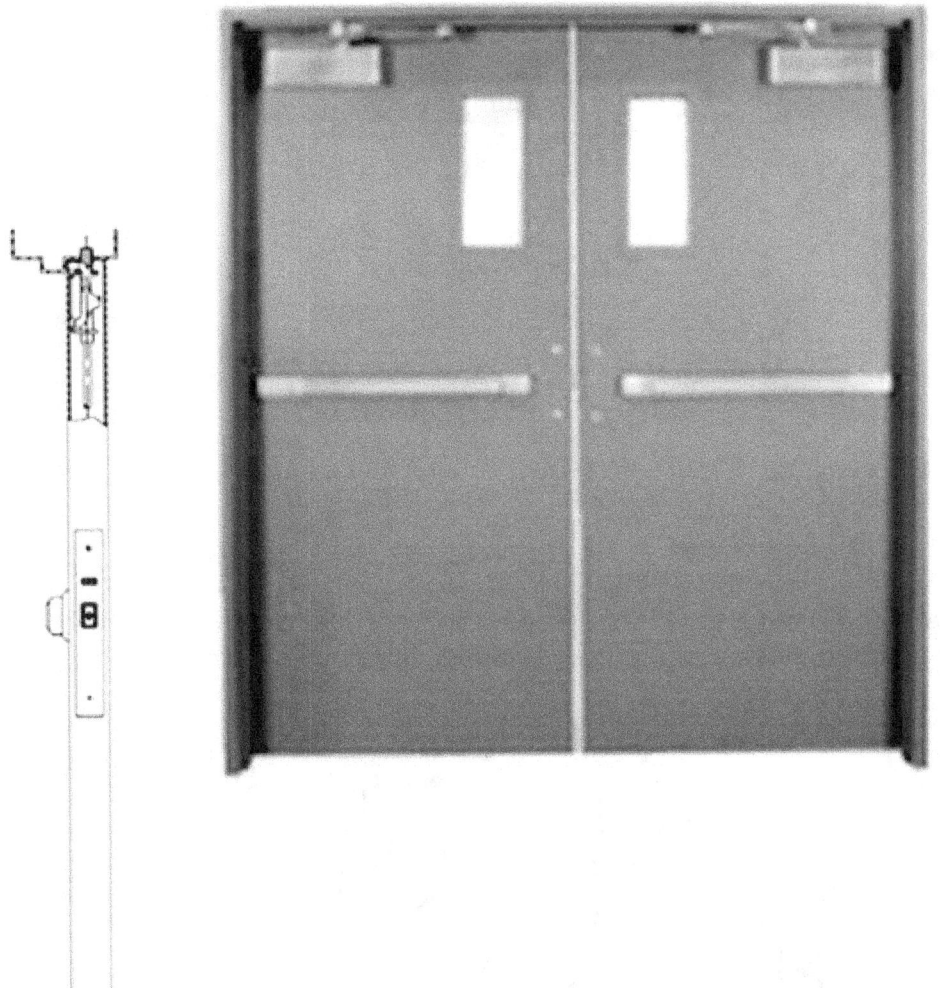

Most 'Top Rod Only Exit' Devices require installation of a fusible link release pin that melts at a high temperature preventing the doors from being blown open by the force of a fire and resulting in a "Backdraft" - essentially an explosion of super-heated air.

Von Duprin recently introduced a concealed vertical rod device that uses a cable instead of a rod to actuate the latches at the top and bottom of the door in their vertical rod device. This is designed to speed installation and resist problems commonly associated with vertical rod devices.

Manufacturers constantly try to improve Exit Devices.

Other options that might affect the series include an inside cylinder dogging device, where the door can be left unlatched by turning a real key in a real cylinder, instead of an Allen (hex) key which is readily available to the public.

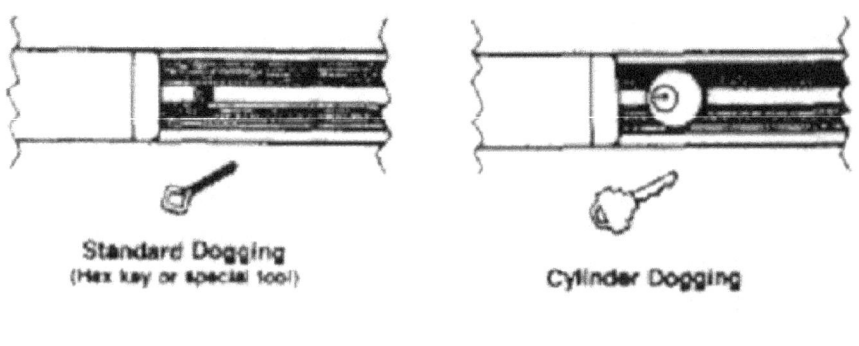

Standard Dogging
(Hex key or special tool)

Cylinder Dogging

Cylinder Dogging

The cylinder may be in the outer escutcheon plate (15b), a door control (16), nowhere (passage) (17) or even on the inside of the device to lock the outside trim.

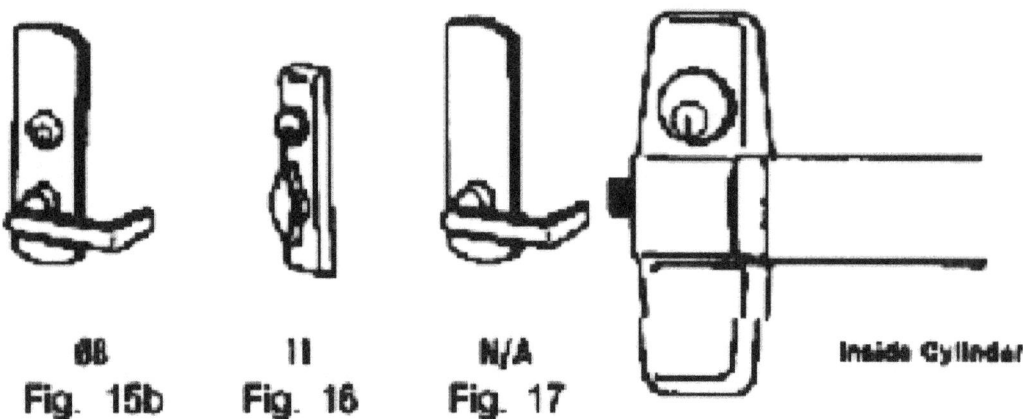

| 08 | 11 | N/A | Inside Cylinder |
| Fig. 15b | Fig. 16 | Fig. 17 | |

Section Eight: Basic Master Keying Terms

bitting depth
n. the depth of a cut which is made into the blade of a key

bitting list
n. a listing of all the key combinations used within a system. The combinations are usually arranged in order of the blind code, direct code, and/or key symbol.

bitting orientation
n. the specification of how a written combination is to be applied to bitting positions of a key (tip-to-bow, etc.)

bitting position
n. the location of a key cut

blind code
n. a designation, unrelated to the bitting, assigned to a particular key combination for future reference when additional keys or cylinders may be needed

change key
n. 1. a key which operates only one cylinder or one group of keyed alike cylinders in a keying system, 2. any device that is used to mechanically or electronically allow resetting of certain key or combination locks, see also "reset key" #1

CK
abb. change key

concealed key control
n. a specification that all keys and the non-visible portion of all lock cylinders be stamped with standard keying symbols

controlled cross keying
n. a condition in which two or more different keys of the same level of keying and under the same higher level key(s) operate one cylinder by design; e.g., XAA1 operated by AA2 (but not XAA1 operated by AB1) Note: This condition could severely limit the security of the cylinder and the maximum expansion of the system when (1) more than a few of these different keys operate a cylinder, or (2) more than a few differently cross keyed cylinders per system are required.

cross keying
n. the deliberate process of combinating a cylinder (usually in a master key system) to two or more different keys which would not normally be expected to operate it together. See also "controlled cross keying" and "uncontrolled cross keying."

CTK
abb. control key

direct code
n. a designation assigned to a particular key which includes the actual combination of the key

display key
n. a special change key in a hotel master key system which will allow access to one designated guest room, even if the lock is in the shut out mode. It may also act as a shut out key for that room.

emergency master key
n. a special master key which usually operates all guestroom locks in a hotel master key system at all times, even in the shut out mode. This key may also act as a shut out key.

EMK
abb. emergency master key

grand master key
n. the key which operates two or more separate groups of locks, which are each operated by a different master key

grand master key system
n. a master key system which has exactly three levels of keying

grand master keyed
adj. of or pertaining to a lock or cylinder which is or is to be keyed into a grand master key system

great grand master key
n. the key which operates two or more separate groups of locks which are each operated by a different grand master key

great grand master key system
n. a master key system which has exactly four levels of keying

great grand master keyed
adj. of or pertaining to a lock or cylinder which is or is to be keyed into a great grand master key system

great great grand master key
n. the key which operates two or more separate groups of locks which are each operated by different great grand master keys

great great grand master key system
n. a master key system which has five or more levels of keying

great great grand master keyed
adj. of or pertaining to a lock or cylinder which is or is to be keyed into a great great grand master key system

GGGMK
abb. great great grand master key

GGGMK'D
abb. great great grand master keyed

GGM
abb. great grand master key

GGMK
abb. great grand master key

GGMK'D
abb. great grand master keyed

GM
abb. grand master key

GMK
abb. grand master key

GMK section
abb. grand master key section

GMK'D
abb. grand master keyed

hotel cylinder
n. a cylinder which can function to prevent the operation of all keys except emergency, display and some shut out keys. It may also contain an indicator.

KA
abb. keyed alike

KA1, KA2, etc.
symbol which indicates that all cylinders so designated are or are to be operated by the same key(s). The numerical designation indicates the keyed alike group or set.

KA/2, KA/3, etc.
symbol used to indicate the quantity of locks or cylinders in keyed alike groups. These groups are usually formed from a larger quantity; e.g., 30 cylinders KA/2.

keyed alike
adj. of or pertaining to two or more looks or cylinders which have or are to have the same combination. They may or may not be part of a keying system

keyed different
adj. of or pertaining to a group of locks or cylinders, each of which is or is to be combinated differently from the others. They may or may not be a part of a keying system.

keyed random
adj. of or pertaining to a cylinder or group of cylinders selected from a limited inventory of different key changes. Duplicate bittings may occur.

Keyed Directly To
applied to locks that are operated by no keys lower than a particular Master Key, Grand Master Key, Great-Grand Master Key, Great-Great-Grand Master Key, etc

key system schematic
n. a drawing with blocks utilizing keying symbols, usually illustrating the hierarchy of all keys within a master key system. It indicates the structure and total expansion of the system.

levels of keying
n. pl. the divisions of a master key system into hierarchies of access, as shown in the following tables. Note: the standard key coding system has been expanded to include key symbols for systems of more than four levels of keying.

TWO LEVEL SYSTEM

LEVEL OF KEYING	KEY NAME	ABB.	KEY SYMBOL
Level II	master key	MK	AA
Level I	change key	CK	1AA, 2AA, etc.

THREE LEVEL SYSTEM

LEVEL OF KEYING	KEY NAME	ABB.	KEY SYMBOL
Level III	grand master key	GMK	A
Level II	master key	MK	AA, AB, etc.
Level I	change key	CK	AA1, AA2, etc

FOUR LEVEL SYSTEM

LEVEL OF KEYING	KEY NAME	ABB.	KEY SYMBOL
Level IV	great grand master key	GGMK	GGMK
Level III	grand master key	GMK	A, B, etc. AA,
Level II	master key	MK	AB, etc. AA1,
Level I	change key	CK	AA2, etc.

FIVE LEVEL SYSTEM

LEVEL OF KEYING	KEY NAME	ABB.	KEY SYMBOL
Level V	great great grand master key	GGGMK	GGGMK
Level IV	great grand master key	GGMK	A, B, etc. AA,
Level III	grand master key	GMK	AB, etc. AAA,
Level II	master key	MK	AAB, etc.
Level I	change key	CK	AAA1, AAA2, etc.

SIX LEVEL SYSTEM

LEVEL OF KEYING	KEY NAME	ABB.	KEY SYMBOL
Level VI	great great grand master key	GGGMK	GGGMK
Level V	great grand master key	GGMK	A, B, etc. AA,
Level IV	grand master key	GMK	AB, etc. AAA,
Level III	master key	MK	AAB, etc.
Level II	sub-master key	SMK	AAAA, AAAB, etc.
Level I	change key	CK	AAAA1, AAAA2, etc.

master keyed only
adj. of or pertaining to a lock or cylinder which is or is to be combinated only to a master key

Maison key system
n. [from the French, meaning "house" key system] a keying system in which one or more cylinders are operated by every key (or relatively large numbers of different keys) in the system; e.g., main entrances of apartment buildings operated by all individual suite keys of the building

master key
n. 1. a key which operates all the master keyed locks or cylinders in a group, each lock or cylinder usually operated by its own change key, 2. v. to combinate a group of locks or cylinders such that each is operated by its own change key as well as by a master key for the entire group, 3. n. an automotive key which operates all or most locks on a vehicle where there is also a valet key employed

Masterkey
(adjective) descriptive of the techniques used to describe such a system, or to describe the system itself.
(verb) apply a master key system to a cylinder or cylinders

master key changes
n. the number of different usable change keys available under a given master key

MK
abb. master key

modified key coding system
n. a modification of the standard key coding system, in which the TMK of a system with three or more levels of keying has a single letter name, and keys at lower levels are named following SKCS conventions

NCK
sym. symbol for "no change key," primarily used in hardware schedules

NMK
abb. a notation used to indicate "not master keyed" and is suffixed in parentheses to a regular keying symbol. It indicates that the cylinder is not to be operated by the master key(s) specified in the regular keying symbol; e.g., AB6(NMK).

shut out key
n. usually used in hotel keying systems, a key which will make the lock inoperative to all other keys in the system except the emergency master key, display key, and some types of shut out keys

shut out mode
n. the state of a hotel function lockset which prevents operation by all keys except the emergency master key, display key, and some types of shut out keys

SKCS
abb. standard key coding system

standard key coding system
n. an industry standard and uniform method of designating all keys and/or cylinders in a master key system. The designation automatically indicates the exact function and keying level of each key and/or cylinder in the system, usually without further explanation.

visual key control
n. a specification that all keys and the visible portion of the front of all lock cylinders be stamped with standard keying symbols

You should also be aware of how the KBA (Key Bitting Array) and the SOP (Sequenced Of Progression affect the layout of the system. The number of positions in each vertical column of the KBA creates the breakdown of the system.

If you are not using a TMK (Top Master Key) cut in any given position of the KBA, that position will have a number of other possibilities which create the pattern. If there are four possibilities, everything will break into groups of 4...4 bittings per Block, 4 Blocks per Column, 4 Columns per Page, 4 Pages per Group, 4 Groups per Section, and 4 Sections per Six Pin System, and 4 Six pin Systems in a Seven Pin System.

Using a Standard Progression Format chart, this puts multiples of four under each hierarchal level of keying.- 4 bittings per block; 16 per column; 64 per page; 156 per group of pages; 1024 per section of 4 groups; 4096 per six pin system; 16,384 per seven pin system.

If you are not using a TMK (Top Master Key) cut in any given position of the KBA, that position will have a number of other possibilities which create the pattern. If there are five possibilities, everything will break into groups of 5...5 bittings per Block, 5 Blocks per Column, 5 Columns per Page, 5 Pages per Group, 5 Groups per Section, and 5 Sections per Six Pin System, and 5 Six pin Systems in a Seven Pin System.

Using a Standard Progression Format chart, this puts multiples of five under each hierarchal level of keying.- 5 bittings per block; 25 per column; 125 per page; 625 per group of pages; 3125 per section of 5 groups; 15,625 per six pin system; 78,125 per seven pin system.

On the other hand, the Sequence Of Progression does not directly affect the math of laying out the system, because the same keys are created regardless of the order in which they appear. The SOP changes the order the keys appear in and can make the system less easy to -crackll visually or predict what key operates a given lock or door.

You will sometimes encounter the term Theoretical Master Key. This is not an approved term under the LIST Council dictionary. It refers to the fact that in some cases a given key is used to develop the system, but cylinders are not pinned to it, nor are any keys cut to it. The main thing for early master keying knowledge is simply to be aware of the term so as to not be confused if it is encountered.

Section Nine: Terms relating to Installation

When a door is purchased, it can come prepared four ways.
1) Blank
2) Basic Template
3) Templated for a particular series of lockset
4) Fully Prepped

Receiving a blank door is rare even with wooden doors and is virtually unheard of with steel clad or steel doors or hollow metal doors. What are these types of doors?

A wooden door can be a hollow core door or a pressboard door, or a solid wood door.

The hollow core door is basically a figure eight frame which may truly be hollow, may be filled with cardboard X's to give it more strength, may be filled with foam or Styrofoam pellets, or may be filled with fire resistant powder.

A pressboard door is the figure eight frame filled with sheets of pressboard or wooden shavings glued together. This is also referred to as a Solid Core Wood Door.

A Solid Wood Door is one made by fitting boards together and gluing and fastening them into what in essence becomes a large solid block of wood.

Solid wood doors are quite pricey compared to the other options and are rarely seen. Hollow core doors are typically used only on interior doors such as residential bedrooms. Filled Hollow Core Doors can be found on offices and stairway doors in large buildings.

Metal doors also come in various types. Describing them as simply as possible, they might be Kalamein doors (not Calamine like the lotion though it is pronounced similarly), Steel doors or Hollow Metal Doors.

Kalamein doors are wooden doors of some sort which are clad on the exterior with a covering of steel. They are usually quite ugly and only typically found in warehouses.

Steel doors are a figure eight frame of wood covered with a wrapping of steel in a given gauge (thickness) with thicker doors being both more pricey and more resistive to problems. They will typically be identifiable on the door edge, where the two halves meet in the middle of the edge of the door and are pressed into a slot in the wood. Common gauges are 24 and 32 gauge.

Hollow metal doors are more solidly built and their frame is of higher quality metal. Typically the framework will meet on one face of the door where it will have been welded together, so where the two halves meet on the edge of the door will be at one of the two faces. Hollow metal doors are also sold in different gauges with better quality ones having a thicker gauge.

An interesting and important thing to note is that the larger the number, the thinner the gauge, so a 12 gauge door is a behemoth and a 32 gauge door is little more than what a low cost residential steel door might be. Common thicknesses are 14 gauge and 16 gauge.

No matter what type of door it is, however, it is rare to see a fully blank door. Most of the time if you do see one it will be on an expensive solid wood door.

Instead, most doors will come with a door preparation (prep) for some type of lock. For residential usage it will likely be either a 160 or 161 prep. The 160 is a prep for medium duty (grades two and three) lockset. The 161 is a prep for medium to heavy duty (grades one and two) lockset, commonly found on commercial doors such as offices and institutions.

Both of these door preparations (preps) use a two and one eighth inch hole through the face of the door. This opening is referred to, as you have seen, referred to as the face bore or cross bore.

The most noticeable difference between them is the backset, or distance from the edge of the door to the center of the face bore. On the 160, it is two and three eighths of an inch, but on the 161 it is two and three quarters of an inch, about a half inch more.

The edge bore and the cutout for the latch face also differ slightly. The 160 prep uses either a 7/8 inch or 15/16 inch edge bore, while the 161 uses a one inch. And the width of the latch face is an eighth of an inch wider on the 161 as well.

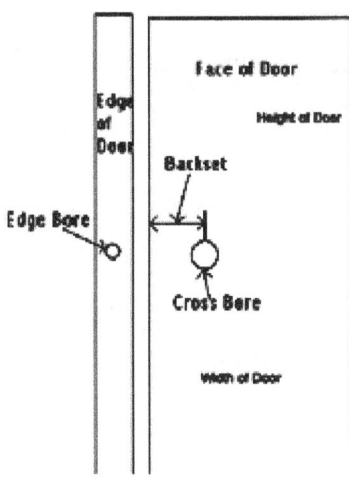

astragal
n. a molding attached to the face of the active leaf of a pair of doors and overlapping the inactive leaf

automatic flush bolt
n. a flush bolt designed to extend itself when both leaves of the pair of doors are in the closed position

auxiliary lock
n. any lock installed in addition to the primary lockset

back plate
n. a thin piece of metal, usually with a concave portion, used with machine screws to fasten certain types of cylinders to a door

backset
n. the distance between the center of a cross-bore and the bolt edge of a door or drawer

bevel (of a door)
n. the pitch on the leading edge of a door which allows clearance for closing

bi-fold door
n. a door with two or more sets of hinges, the additional set(s) allows the door to have an accordion action when opened

boring jig
n. a tool, temporarily affixed to a door, which provides a template structure to guide drill bits properly when preparing for the installation of specific hardware

circular strike
n. a typically round, finished strike, usually driven into place in a drilled hole

cross-bore
n. a hole drilled into the face of a door where a bored or interconnected lockset is to be installed

door bumper
n. an obstruction installed to prevent a door or lock from contacting another object

door silencer
n. a bumper installed in the jamb stop to quiet the closing of a door

drive-in
adj. pertaining to a latch or bolt with a round face

dust box
n. an enclosure applied under a strike to enhance appearance and/or performance

dust proof strike
n. a typically floor mounted strike that has a spring loaded internal plunger designed to keep the receptacle free of dust and debris

edge-bore
n. a hole drilled into the edge of a door where a bored or interconnected lockset is to be installed

effective throw
n. the distance a deadlatch remains projected when the guard bolt has been engaged and end pressure is applied to the latch

escutcheon
n. a surface mounted trim which enhances the appearance and/or security of a lock installation

extension link
n. a device which is used to extend the backset of a spring latch or dead latch

face plate
n. the finished, removable plate which covers the front of some locks

filler plate
n. a usually flat piece of material used to; cover a hole or opening, provide a foundation for mounting additional hardware, or adjust the position of hardware as mounted

finish
n. a material, coloring and/or texturing specification

French doors
n. a set of double doors composed of many small glass panes and narrow stiles

full mortise
adj. pertaining to a method of installation in which only the faceplate and trim is exposed. The lock case is installed in a pocket in the door or drawer v. to make a rectangular pocket in a door or drawer that is only open on the edge of the door or drawer

function
n. a set of operating features for a particular type of lock or exit device which make it suitable for a specific application. The function is designated by a classification name or standards reference number. See ANSI or BHMA for a \specific listing.

handed
adj. pertaining to hardware which is manufactured only for application on doors with a specific orientation

header
n. the horizontal, top, member of a door jamb

hinge security stud
n. a protrusion on one leaf of a hinge which interlocks with the other when the door is closed

hinge stile
n. the vertical edge of a door where hinges are installed

hold open
n. 1. a function of self-latching hardware which allows a lock to be set in a non-latching mode 2. A function of a door closer, or separate hardware device, which allows the door to be retained in an open position

hollow core door
n. a non-metal door with structural reinforcement creating air pockets between the two faces

hollow metal door
n. typically a door made of sheet metal on all surfaces and lightly reinforced to make it rigid

jamb
n. the vertical components of a door frame

Kalamein door
n. a metal clad door that has a wood filler

kick plate
n. a protective plate mounted on the bottom of a door to prevent damage to minimize damage to the door

latch
1. n. a mechanical or magnetic door fastener which can automatically keep a door, gate, etc., closed, 2. v. engagement of a latch when a door, gate, etc. is pushed or pulled closed

latch bolt
n. a spring actuated bolt, normally with one or more beveled surfaces, which, when aligned with the strike, engages it automatically

latch guard
n. a plate or combination of interlocking pieces designed to block access to the edge of a latch when the door is shut

latch tube
n. the encasement portion of some types of lockset that contains the latch and may also contain its operating mechanism

lock stile
n. the vertical edge of a door designed for lock or latch installation

medium stile
adj. pertaining to an aluminum or hollow metal door with a stile generally between 3-1/4 and 4-1/4 inches wide

mop plate
n. A narrow plate fixed to the bottom of a door for protection against soiling from a mop; similar to a kickplate

mortise
1. v. to prepare by removing stock material from the edge of a door, drawer, frame or opening to create a recess which allows the flush fit or insetting of relevant lock or other hardware, 2. n. the cavity prepared by mortising, 3. adj. of or pertaining to a locking device designed to fit in a mortise preparation

narrow stile
adj. pertaining to aluminum doors with stiles generally between 1-3/4 and 2-3/4 inches wide

peep hole
n. a small lens or opening which allows a limited view through a door

pitcher handle
n. lock trim which serves as a pull and is generally perpendicular to the door at its top mount, then bends and tapers to its bottom mount

prep
n. 1. the location and dimensions of the cut out(s) and reinforcing in a door or frame required to accept a piece of hardware. 2. v. to prepare a door or frame for installation of a lock or other hardware

push plate
n. a generally flat and commonly rectangular trim mounted for hand contact to push open a door

pull handle
n. trim for gripping to apply pulling force to a door

pull plate
n. a generally flat and commonly rectangular trim with an attached handle for pulling open a door

push plate
n. a generally flat and commonly rectangular trim mounted for hand contact to push open a door

single acting (door)
n. a door which swings from the latched position in only one direction

split astragal
n. an astragal constructed of two pieces; each piece being mounted on either door of the pair, and abutting to create a seal

split finish
adj. of or pertaining to a lockset whose finish is different on each side of the door

split hub
n. a two-piece hub which can allow motion from one side of a swivel spindle while preventing it from the other side

split spindle
n. a multi-piece spindle which allows a knob or lever to be installed on only one side of a door

spring latch
n. a latch operated under spring pressure, having no deadlatching feature

square corner latch
n. a latch with a face whose sides meet at 90 degree angles

stile
n. the vertical construction member located on either edge of a door

stop (of a door)
n. the projecting portion of a doorframe upon which the door rests when closed

store door function
n. a lockset function in which: a) a deadbolt is operated by key from either side and a latch is operated by working trim from either side; or b) a deadlocking latch can be withdrawn by working trim from either side except when both sides are locked by key from either side.

strike
n. a bolt receptacle typically mounted in the door jamb or the floor

strike locator
n. a tool used to mark the jamb, relative to the bolt of the lock, prior to strike installation

strike reinforcer
n. a metal plate mounted behind a strike, using long screws to secure it to the door frame

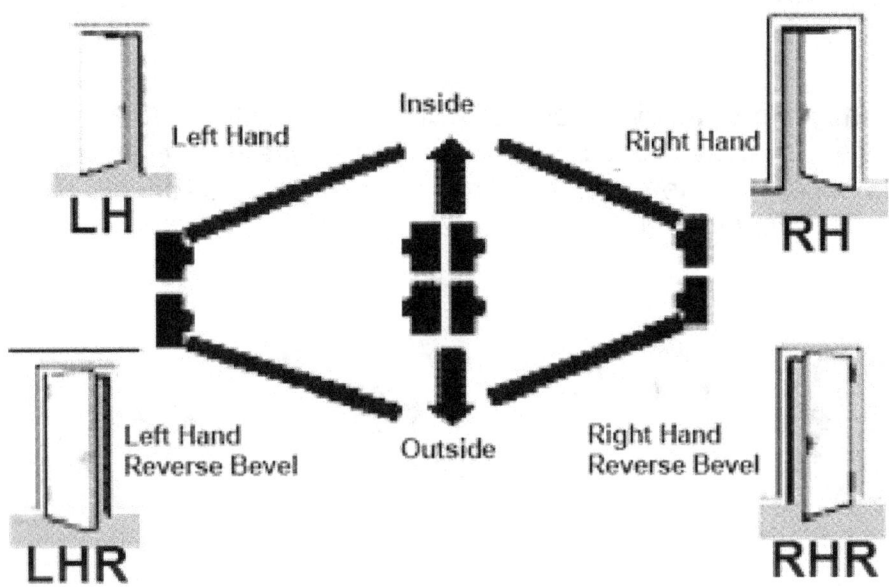

Note: When purchasing doors from a retail location be aware that many box stores do not use proper terminology. A -Right Hand Outswing‖ in these retailers is actually a Left Hand Reverse, and a -Left Hand Outswing‖ is actually a Right Hand Reverse.

Section Ten: Utility Lock Terms

In a typical disc tumbler mechanism, each wafer (or disc) is pushed outward to extend beyond the plug shearline by a small spring pushing against its -flag‖ or -leg‖. The key enters the large open square in the center of the tumbler, and pushes in the direction opposite to that of the spring.

In some lock cylinders, such as foreign auto locks, some springs may push one way and others the opposite direction, resulting in keys which require cuts on more than one surface of the key.

Keys like these might be -double-sided‖ or truly -double-bitted‖. If the key is cut on more than one side for convenience only, it is -double-sided‖, but if it is cut on more than one side to accommodate tumblers arranged similarly, it is -double-bitted‖. Either way, it can be called -double-cut‖.

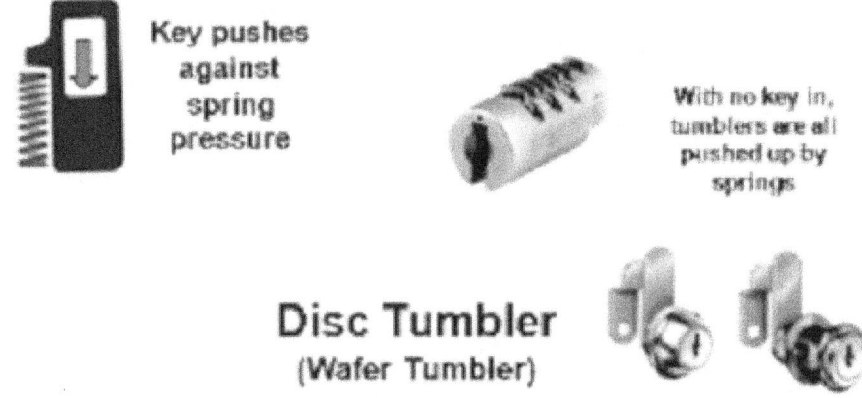

cam
n. 1. a lock or cylinder component which transfers the rotational motion of a key or cylinder plug to the bolt works of a lock 2. the bolt of a cam lock

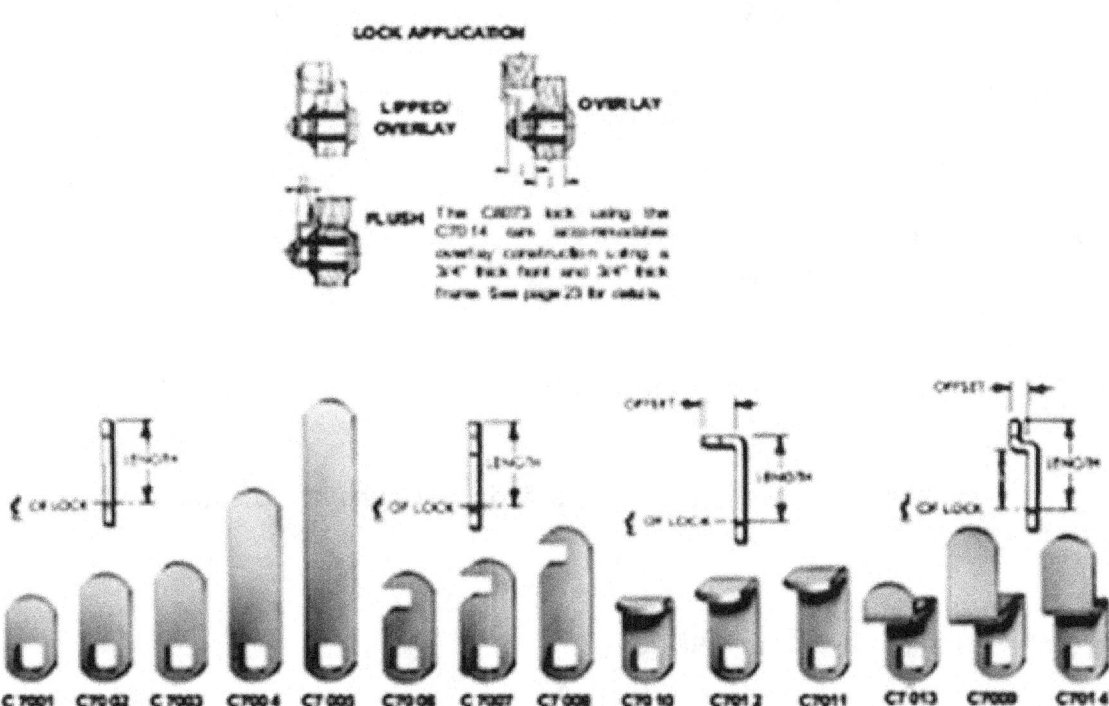

Flat Key

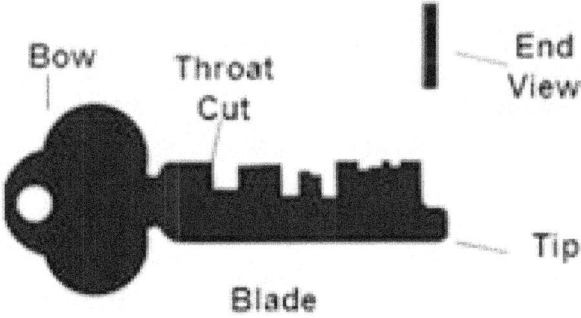

Flat keys are commonly found on inexpensive furniture locks, inside doors in business safes or on Bank Safety Deposit Box locks. Almost all of the locks they operate are of the lever type.

General Terminology for Utility Locks

diamond back
adj. pertaining to a rim cabinet lock whose mounting flanges and case forms the general shape of a diamond

double bitted key
n. a key typically bitted on two opposite surfaces

double cut
1. n. two bittings for the same tumbler position 2. adj. see "double bitted key"

double-D
n . a shape consisting of two opposing arcs and two opposing flats adj. 2. Having such a shape.

double-D punch
n. a tool used to make a double-D hole

dust cover
n. a device designed to prevent foreign matter from entering a mechanism through the keyway

dustproof cylinder
n. a cylinder designed to prevent foreign matter from entering either end of the keyway

frangible shackle
n. a padlock shackle designed to be broken easily

frangible shackle padlock
n. a padlock equipped with an easily broken shackle

key pull(s)
n. a lock specification which indicates by quantity and orientation the position(s) in which a key may be withdrawn

key pull position
n. any position, of the cylinder plug at which the key can be removed

key retaining
adj. 1. of or pertaining to a lock which must be locked before its key can be removed. 2. of or pertaining to a cylinder or lock which may prevent removal of a key without the use of an additional key and/or tool

lazy cam/tailpiece
n. a cam or tailpiece designed to remain stationary while the cylinder plug is partially rotated and/or vice-versa

lever tumbler
n. a flat, spring-loaded tumbler which usually pivots on a post. It contains a gate which must be aligned with a fence to allow movement of the bolt.

pop out lock
n. a plunger lock usually used on vending machines to prevent operation of a T-handle

removable shackle
adj. referring to a type of padlock which is unlocked by removing the shackle from the case

shackle
n. 1. the part of a padlock, which passes through an opening in an object or fits around an object and is ultimately locked into the case 2. the portion of a restraint which fits around the wrist, ankle, neck, waist or thumb

shackle retaining pin
n. a pin which keeps an unlocked shackle heel in the case

shackle spring
n. a spring which pushes the shackle into the open position when the padlock is unlocked

showcase lock
n. normally a ratchet lock or plunger lock used on bypassing doors

shrouded shackle
n. a shackle which is protected from cutting or tampering by design or by the use of secondary shields

single-D
adj. the shape of a cutout for a lock, circular except for a flat section on one side

staple
n. the portion of a hasp assembly with the hole or opening to receive a padlock

wafer tumbler
n. 1. a flat tumbler which must be drawn into the cylinder plug by the proper key so that none of its extremities extends into the shell 2. a flat, usually rectangular tumbler with a gate which must be aligned with a sidebar by the proper key

rabbeted door
n. a door having and edge contoured with an offset creating two surfaces which form an overlap at the abutting edge

reveal
n. the distance measured from the trim surface of the jamb to the leading face of the door on the stop side when closed

reverse bevel
adj. pertaining to the bevel of a door which swings towards the outside

reverse strike
n. a strike used for rim mounted hardware used on reverse bevel doors

reversible
adj. pertaining to hardware that is manufactured in a way, which allows field assembly or adjustment to accommodate installation on doors with different orientations

right hand reverse bevel (door)
adj. pertaining to a right handed door which swings outward

round back
adj. pertaining to a rim cabinet lock whose mounting flanges and case form the general shape of a circle when viewed from the back

round cornered latch
adj. of or pertaining to a latch mounting plate with radiused corners

scalp
n. a thin piece of metal which is usually crimped or spun onto the front of a cylinder. It determines the cylinder's finish and may also serve as the plug retainer.

sex bolt
n. a nut and bolt set used to through bolt, with a closed nut basically flush with the mounting surface creating the appearance of a carriage bolt

lazy cam/tailpiece
n. a cam or tailpiece designed to remain stationary while the cylinder plug is partially rotated and/or vice-versa

lever tumbler
n. a flat, spring-loaded tumbler which usually pivots on a post. It contains a gate which must be aligned with a fence to allow movement of the bolt.

pop out lock
n. a plunger lock usually used on vending machines to prevent operation of a T-handle

removable shackle
adj. referring to a type of padlock which is unlocked by removing the shackle from the case

shackle
n. 1. the part of a padlock, which passes through an opening in an object or fits around an object and is ultimately locked into the case 2. the portion of a restraint which fits around the wrist, ankle, neck, waist or thumb

shackle retaining pin
n. a pin which keeps an unlocked shackle heel in the case

shackle spring
n. a spring which pushes the shackle into the open position when the padlock is unlocked

showcase lock
n. normally a ratchet lock or plunger lock used on bypassing doors

shrouded shackle
n. a shackle which is protected from cutting or tampering by design or by the use of secondary shields

single-D
adj. the shape of a cutout for a lock, circular except for a flat section on one side

staple
n. the portion of a hasp assembly with the hole or opening to receive a padlock

wafer tumbler
n. 1. a flat tumbler which must be drawn into the cylinder plug by the proper key so that none of its extremities extends into the shell 2. a flat, usually rectangular tumbler with a gate which must be aligned with a sidebar by the proper key

rabbeted door
n. a door having and edge contoured with an offset creating two surfaces which form an overlap at the abutting edge

reveal
n. the distance measured from the trim surface of the jamb to the leading face of the door on the stop side when closed

reverse bevel
adj. pertaining to the bevel of a door which swings towards the outside

reverse strike
n. a strike used for rim mounted hardware used on reverse bevel doors

reversible
adj. pertaining to hardware that is manufactured in a way, which allows field assembly or adjustment to accommodate installation on doors with different orientations

right hand reverse bevel (door)
adj. pertaining to a right handed door which swings outward

round back
adj. pertaining to a rim cabinet lock whose mounting flanges and case form the general shape of a circle when viewed from the back

round cornered latch
adj. of or pertaining to a latch mounting plate with radiused corners

scalp
n. a thin piece of metal which is usually crimped or spun onto the front of a cylinder. It determines the cylinder's finish and may also serve as the plug retainer.

sex bolt
n. a nut and bolt set used to through bolt, with a closed nut basically flush with the mounting surface creating the appearance of a carriage bolt

Section Eleven: Warning Signs

Radiation
(red on yellow)

Bio Safety Hazard
(Black on Orange)

Laser
(white on red and black on white)

High Magnetic Field
(Black on orange and yellow)

The locksmith should always be on the alert for hazardous warning signs and learn what caused them to be placed there. Otherwise, the locksmith could easily be injured, killed or cause injury to someone else.

The danger level or risk level of a biohazard is a numerical indicator from 1 to 4, with **4** being the most dangerous and infectious. There is a level 5, but the risk is so high that no one can enter the area without the proper training and equipment. (The e-bola research area at the CDC lab would be an example of a level 5 biohazard).

There are many other types of hazards, such as chemical, electrical, and radio wave radiation that the institutional locksmith must be aware of. OSHA (Occupational Safety and Health Administration) has set standards which use four words to advise you of dangers.

NOTICE

Use this when you want to indicate a statement of company policy as the message relates directly or indirectly to the safety of personnel or protection of property.

CAUTION

Use this when there is a hazardous situation where minor or moderate injury could result. A Caution worded sign should not be used where there is the possibility of death or severe injury.

WARNING

Use this when there is a hazardous situation where the probability of death or severe injury exists.

DANGER

Use this when there is a hazardous situation where there is a high probability of death or severe injury.

Chapter Twelve: Abbreviations and Acronyms

We pretty much all know what an abbreviation is. It is a letter or group of letters used as a shortened form of a word or phrase. Robert Parker, for example, might abbreviate his name to R. Parker. In the united States, we almost always use an abbreviation for our middle names on documents. We commonly see the abbreviation -abbr used for the word -abbreviation, or ST for Street

Acronyms, on the other hand, are a more specific form of abbreviation.
Random House Dictionary defines an acronym as:

acronym ac·ro·nym [ak-ruh-nim]
noun 1. a word formed from the initial letters or groups of letters of words in a set phrase or series of words, as WAC from Women's Army Corps, or OPEC from Organization of Petroleum Exporting Countries.

Acronyms are frequently, but not always, capitalized.

On top of that are specialized acronyms. Most acronyms refer to a group, but some are Certifications. In our listings here, if it is a certification acronym it will be indicated by (certification) instead of (acronym).

And while some simple abbreviations are technically acronyms because they use the first letters of the words, the (acronym) will only appear here for acronyms of groups.

If it is an abbreviation (even if technically also an acronym, but not for a group) we will try to break it down into the type of usage. If it is a master keying related term, it will be marked (master keying); If commonly used in reference to lock installation, (lock installation) will be indicated.

Sometimes more than one such usage will be listed for a term. For example, a -161 prepll refers to a cutout in the door made to allow installation of a lock. So the term refers to the door parts and also to installation terms. So it would be marked (door) (installation). The use of separate parenthesis for each usage is to avoid confusion. If it were instead marked (door installation) for example, the reader might think it refers to installing a door.

The following is a list of the abbreviations and acronyms used in the LIST (an acronym for Lock Industry Standards and Training) Council Dictionary. After each one, we have added, in parenthesis, a brief description of where it is commonly used or whether it is an acronym.

FULL LIST OF ABBREVIATIONS AND ACRONYMS from LIST Council Dictionary

A, AA, AA1, 1AA, etc.
key symbol - see also standard key coding system
(master keying)(keys)

ADA
abb. Americans with Disabilities Act
(acronym) (Life Safety)

AED
abb. anti-explosive device
(basic safe work)

AFTE
abb. Association of Firearm and Toolmark Examiners
(acronym)

AHC
abb. Architectural Hardware Consultant (as certified by DHI)
(acronym)(Certification)

AHD
abb. after hours depository
(basic safe work)

AHJ
abb. authority having jurisdiction
(acronym) (Life Safety)

ALOA
abb. Associated Locksmiths of America, Inc.
(acronym)

ANSI
abb. American National Standards Institute
(acronym)(Life Safety)

ASA
American Standards Association - See ANSI
(acronym)

ASIS
abb. American Society for Industrial Security
(acronym)

ASTM
abb. American Society for Testing and Materials
(acronym)

ATM
abb. automatic teller machine
(basic safe work)

ATT
abb. attendant's key
(master keying)

BBC
abb. Basic Building Code
(acronym)

BCH
abb. bolt control handle
(basic safe work)

BHMA
abb. Builders Hardware Manufacturers Association
(acronym)

BM
abb. block master key
(master keying)

BMK
abb. block master key
(master keying)

BOCA
abb. Building Officials and Code Administration International - formerly Basic Building Code
(acronym)

CAL
abb. the title "Certified Automotive Locksmith" as awarded by ALOA
(Certification)

CAN
abb. controller area network
(electronics, electromechanical, access control and computers)

CBOK
abb. construction breakout key
(master keying)

CCW
abb. Counter Clockwise, as used in combination dialing instructions
(basic safe work)

CICC
abb. contactless smart card
(electronics, electromechanical, access control and computers)

CIL
abb. the title "Certified Institutional Locksmith" as awarded by ILA
(Certification)

CJIL
abb. the title "Certified Journeyman Institutional Locksmith" as awarded by ILA
(Certification)

CJL
abb. the title Certified Journeyman Locksmith as awarded by the Professional Locksmith Association of Alberta
(Certification)

CJS
abb. the title "Certified Journeyman Safecracker" as awarded by NSO
(Certification)

CK
abb. change key
(master keying)(pinning)

CMIL
abb. the title "Certified Master Institutional Locksmith" as awarded by ILA
(Certification)

CMK
abb. construction master key
(master keying)(pinning)

CMK'd
abb. construction master keyed
(master keying)(pinning)

CMKS
abb. the title "Certified Master Keying Specialist" as awarded by ILA
(Certification) (master keying)

CML
abb. the title "Certified Master Locksmith" as awarded by ALOA
(Certification)

CMS
abb. the title "Certified Master Safecracker" as awarded by NSO
(Certification)

CMST
abb. the title "Certified Master Safe Technician" as awarded by SAVTA
(Certification)

CO
abb. certificate of occupancy
(Life Safety)

CPL
abb. the title "Certified Professional Locksmith" as awarded by ALOA
(Certification)

CPP
abb. the title "Certified Protection Professional" as awarded by ASIS
(Certification)

CPS
abb. the title "Certified Professional Safe Technician" as awarded by SAVTA
(Certification)

CRL
abb. the title "Certified Registered Locksmith" as awarded by ALOA
(Certification)

CSI
abb. Construction Specifiers Institute
(acronym)

CTK
abb. Control Key, used on pinning charts
(master keying)

CTRL
abb. control key
(master keying)

CW
abb. Clockwise, as used in combination dialing instructions
(basic safe work)

DHI
abb. Door and Hardware Institute
(acronym)

EAC
abb. electronic access control
(electronics, electromechanical, access control and computers)

ECM
abb. engine control module
(automotive)

EIA
abb. Electronics Industry Association
(acronym) (electronics, electromechanical, access control and computers)

EMK
abb. emergency master key
(master keying)

ENG
abb. engineer's key
(master keying)

ERD
abb. external relocking device
(basic safe work)

FAR
abb. false acceptance rate
(electronics, electromechanical, access control and computers)

FCC ID
abb. Federal Communications Commission Identification
(acronym) (electronics, electromechanical, access control and computers)

FRR
abb. false rejection rate
(electronics, electromechanical, access control and computers)

GGGMK
abb. great great grand master key
(master keying)

GGGMK'D
abb. great great grand master keyed
(master keying)((pinning)

GGM
abb. great grand master key
(master keying)

GGMK
abb. great grand master key
(master keying)

GGMK'D
abb. great grand master keyed
(master keying)(pinning)

GM
abb. grand master key
(master keying)

GMK
abb. grand master key
(master keying)

GMK section
abb. grand master key section
(master keying)

GMK'D
abb. grand master keyed
(master keying)(pinning)

GSA
abb. General Services Administration (US Government)
(acronym) (basic safe work)

HGM
abb. horizontal group master key
(master keying)

HiCo
abb. high coercivity
(electronics, electromechanical, access control and computers)

HKP
abb. housekeeper's key
(master keying)

HM
abb Horizontal Master Key - see also HGM,HMK
(master keying)

HMK
abb Horizontal Master Key – see also HGM,HM
(master keying)

HP
abb. hardplate
(basic safe work)

IC
abb. interchangeable core
(master keying)(cylinders and cores)(pinning)

ICC
International Code Conference (see also ICBO)
(acronym)

ICBO
abb. International Conference of Building Officials – see also ICC
(acronym)

IFDC
abb. "Institutional Fire Door Consultant"; a locksmith certification program administered by ILA
(Certification)

IFDI
abb. "Institutional Fire Door Inspector"; a locksmith certification program administered by ILA
(Certification)

IHC
abb. "Institutional Hardware Consultant"; a locksmith certification program administered by ILA
(Certification)

ILA
abb. Institutional Locksmiths Association
(acronym)

ILCP
abb. "Institutional Locksmith Certification Program"; a locksmith certification program administered by ILA
(acronym)

IP
abb. internet protocol
(electronics, electromechanical, access control and computers)

IR
abb. Infrared
(electronics, electromechanical, access control and computers)

IRD
abb. internal relocking device
(basic safe work)

JIS
abb. Japanese Industrial Standard
(acronym) (basic safe work)

k
sym. symbol for "keys" used after a numerical designation of the quantity of the keys requested to be supplied with the cylinders; e.g., lk, 2k, 3k, etc. it is usually found in hardware/keying schedules.
(master keying)(keys)

KA
abb. keyed alike
(master keying)(pinning)

KA1, KA2, etc.
symbol which indicates that all cylinders so designated are or are to be operated by the same key(s). The numerical designation indicates the keyed alike group or set.
(master keying)(pinning)

KA/2, KA/3, etc.
symbol used to indicate the quantity of locks or cylinders in keyed alike groups. These groups are usually formed from a larger quantity; e.g., 30 cylinders KA/2.
(master keying)(pinning)(lock types)

KBA
abb. key bitting array
(master keying)

KD
abb. keyed different
(master keying)(pinning)

KIK
abb. Key-in-Knob
(lock types)

KIL
abb. Key-in-Lever
(lock types)

KR
abb. 1. keyed random 2. key retaining
(pinning)

KWY
abb. keyway
(master keying)(keys)

LFIC
abb. Large Format Interchangeable Core
(master keying)(cylinders and cores)(pinning)

LH
abb. left hand
(basic safe work)(doors)

LHR
abb. left hand reverse bevel
(doors)(Life Safety)

LLC
Limited Liability Company
(business)

LPP
abb. Limited Position Progression
(master keying)

LM
abb. Line Master Key see also RM, Row Master Key
(master keying)

LHVD
abb. left hand vertical down
(basic safe work)

LHVU
abb. left hand vertical up
(basic safe work)

LOBC
abb. 1. locked on by combination, 2. (sic) locked on back cover
(basic safe work)

LoCo
abb. low coercivity
(electronics, electromechanical, access control and computers)

LRC
abb. Limited Rotating Constant
(master keying)

MACS
abb. maximum adjacent cut specification
(master keying)(key cutting)(keys)

MCCS
Abb. Maximum Compound Cut Specification
(master keying)(key cutting)(keys)

MK
abb. master key
(master keying)(keys)

MKCS
abb. modified key coding system
(master keying)

MK'd
abb. master keyed
(master keying)(cylinders and cores)(pinning)

MK'd only
abb. master keyed only
(master keying)(cylinders and cores)(pinning)

MK section
abb. master key section
(master keying)(cylinders and cores)(keys)

MOCS
abb. maximum opposing cut specification
(master keying)(cylinders and cores)(keys)

MP
abb. manipulation proof
(basic safe work)

MR
abb. manipulation resistant
(basic safe work)

MS
abb. Maximum Security. A trademark of the Adams Rite Manufacturing Co.
(lock types)

NCK
sym. symbol for "no change key," primarily used in hardware schedules
(master keying)(pinning)

NFS
abb. non-fail safe
(electronics, electromechanical, access control and computers)

NKR
abb. non key retaining
(utility locks)

NLSA
abb. National Locksmith Suppliers Association (see also SHDA)
(acronym)

NMK
abb. a notation used to indicate "not master keyed" and is suffixed in parentheses to a regular keying symbol. It indicates that the cylinder is not to be operated by the master key(s) specified in the regular keying symbol; e.g., AB6(NMK).
(master keying)(pinning)

NRK
abb. non-removable key
(utility locks)

NRP
abb. non-removable pin
(hinges)(Life Safety)(doors)

NSO
abb. National Safemans Organization
(acronym)

NSP
abb. National Service Provider
(acronym)

NUR
abb. nurse's key
(master keying)

O.b.
abb. operated by, as used in keying schedules
(master keying)(pinning)

Oe
abb. oersted
(electronics, electromechanical, access control and computers)

PATS
abb. Passive Anti-Theft System
(automotive)

PIN
abb. personal identification number
(electronics, electromechanical, access control and computers)

PIR
abb. passive infra-red
(electronics, electromechanical, access control and computers)

PRP
abb. "Proficiency Registration Program"; a locksmith certification program administered by ALOA
(acronym)

RCM
abb. Rotating Constant Method
(master keying)

RF
abb. Radio Frequency
(electronics, electromechanical, access control and computers)

RFID
abb. radio frequency identification
(electronics, electromechanical, access control and computers)

RH
abb. right-hand
(basic safe work)(doors)(Life Safety)

RHR
abb. (right hand reverse bevel)
(doors)(Life Safety)

RHVD
abb. right hand vertical down
(basic safe work)

RHVU
abb. right hand vertical up
(basic safe work)

RL
abb. The title "Registered Locksmith" as awarded by ALOA
(Certification)

RLD
abb. relocking device
(basic safe work)

RLT
abb. relock trigger
(basic safe work)

RM
abb. row master key
(master keying)

RST
abb. the title "Registered Safe Technician" as awarded by NSO
(Certification)

S/A
abb. sub-assembled
(cylinders and cores)

SAVTA
abb. Safe and Vault Technicians Association
(acronym)

SBCCI
abb. Southern Building Code Congress International
(acronym)

SDB
abb. safe deposit box
(basic safe work)

SFIC
abb. Small Format Interchangeable Core
(master keying)(cylinders and cores)(pinning)(keys)

SHDA
abb. Security Hardware Distributors Association (formerly NLSA)
(acronym)

SKCS
abb. standard key coding system
(master keying)

SKD
sym. symbol for "single keyed", normally followed by a numerical designation in the standard key coding system; e.g., SKD1, SKD2, etc. It indicates that a cylinder or lock is not master keyed but is part of the keying system
(master keying)(pinning)

SMK
abb. sub-master key
(master keying)(keys)

SMNA
abb. Safe Manufacturers' National Association
(acronym)

SOP
abb. Sequence of Progression
(master keying)

STPRP
abb. "Safe Technicians Proficiency Registration Program"; the certification program of SAVTA as administered by ALOA
(acronym)

t-b
abb. tip-to-bow
(keys)(pinning)(cylinders and cores)(master keying)

TCP
abb. transmission control protocol
(electronics, electromechanical, access control and computers)

TCP/IP
n. the system networks use to communicate with one another
(electronics, electromechanical, access control and computers)

TMK
abb. top master key
(master keying)(pinning)

TPP
abb. Total Position Progression
(master keying)

TTL
abb. 1. transistor transistor logic, 2. time to live
(electronics, electromechanical, access control and computers)

UL
abb. Underwriters Laboratories
(acronym) (electronics, electromechanical, access control and computers)

VATS
abb. Vehicle Anti-Theft System
(automotive)

VD
abb. vertical down
(basic safe work)

VGM
abb. vertical group master key see also VM
(master keying)

VKC
abb. visual key control
(master keying)

VM
abb. vertical master key see also VGM
(master keying)

VU
abb. vertical up
(basic safe work)

X
sym. symbol used in hardware schedules to indicate a cross-keyed condition for a particular cylinder; e.g., XAA2, XIX (but not AX7)
(master keying)(pinning)

Now that the full list is shown, let's break it down into usage groups.

Acronyms

ADA
abb. Americans with Disabilities Act
(acronym) (Life Safety)

AFTE
abb. Association of Firearm and Toolmark Examiners
(acronym)

AHC
abb. Architectural Hardware Consultant (as certified by DHI)
(acronym)(Certification)

AHJ
abb. authority having jurisdiction
(acronym) (Life Safety)

ALOA
abb. Associated Locksmiths of America, Inc.
(acronym)

ANSI
abb. American National Standards Institute
(acronym)(Life Safety)

ASA
American Standards Association - See ANSI
(acronym)

ASIS
abb. American Society for Industrial Security
(acronym)

ASTM
abb. American Society for Testing and Materials
(acronym)

BBC
abb. Basic Building Code
(acronym)

BHMA
abb. Builders Hardware Manufacturers Association
(acronym)

BOCA
abb. Building Officials and Code Administration International - formerly Basic Building Code
(acronym)

CSI
abb. Construction Specifiers Institute
(acronym)

DHI
abb. Door and Hardware Institute
(acronym)

EIA
abb. Electronics Industry Association
(acronym) (electronics, electromechanical, access control and computers)

FCC ID
abb. Federal Communications Commission Identification
(acronym) (electronics, electromechanical, access control and computers)

GSA
abb. General Services Administration (US Government)
(acronym) (basic safe work)

ICC
International Code Conference (see also ICBO)
(acronym)

ICBO
abb. International Conference of Building Officials – see also ICC
(acronym)

ILA
abb. Institutional Locksmiths Association
(acronym)

ILCP
abb. "Institutional Locksmith Certification Program"; a locksmith certification program administered by ILA
(acronym)

JIS
abb. Japanese Industrial Standard
(acronym) (basic safe work)

NLSA
abb. National Locksmith Suppliers Association (see also SHDA)
(acronym)

NSO
abb. National Safemans Organization
(acronym)

NSP
abb. National Service Provider
(acronym)

PRP
abb. "Proficiency Registration Program"; a locksmith certification program administered by ALOA
(acronym)

SAVTA
abb. Safe and Vault Technicians Association
(acronym)

SBCCI
abb. Southern Building Code Congress International
(acronym)

SHDA
abb. Security Hardware Distributors Association (formerly NLSA)
(acronym)

SMNA
abb. Safe Manufacturers' National Association
(acronym)

STPRP
abb. "Safe Technicians Proficiency Registration Program"; the certification program of SAVTA as administered by ALOA
(acronym)

UL
abb. Underwriters Laboratories
(acronym) (electronics, electromechanical, access control and computers)

Acronyms for Certifications

AHC
abb. Architectural Hardware Consultant (as certified by DHI)
(acronym)(Certification)

AHJ
abb. authority having jurisdiction
(acronym) (Life Safety)

CAL
abb. the title "Certified Automotive Locksmith" as awarded by ALOA
(Certification)

CIL
abb. the title "Certified Institutional Locksmith" as awarded by ILA
(Certification)

CJIL
abb. the title "Certified Journeyman Institutional Locksmith" as awarded by ILA
(Certification)

CJL
abb. the title Certified Journeyman Locksmith as awarded by the Professional Locksmith Association of Alberta
(Certification)

CJS
abb. the title "Certified Journeyman Safecracker" as awarded by NSO
(Certification)

CMIL
abb. the title "Certified Master Institutional Locksmith" as awarded by ILA
(Certification)

CMKS
abb. the title "Certified Master Keying SpecialistII as awarded by ILA
(Certification) (master keying)

CML
abb. the title "Certified Master Locksmith" as awarded by ALOA
(Certification)

CMS

abb. the title "Certified Master Safecracker" as awarded by NSO
(Certification)

CMST
abb. the title "Certified Master Safe Technician" as awarded by SAVTA
(Certification)

CPL
abb. the title "Certified Professional Locksmith" as awarded by ALOA
(Certification)

CPP
abb. the title "Certified Protection Professional" as awarded by ASIS
(Certification)

CPS
abb. the title "Certified Professional Safe Technician" as awarded by SAVTA
(Certification)

CRL
abb. the title "Certified Registered Locksmith" as awarded by ALOA
(Certification)

IFDC
abb. "Institutional Fire Door Consultant"; a locksmith certification program administered by ILA
(Certification)

IFDI
abb. "Institutional Fire Door Inspector"; a locksmith certification program administered by ILA
(Certification)

IHC
abb. "Institutional Hardware Consultant"; a locksmith certification program administered by ILA
(Certification)

ILCP
abb. "Institutional Locksmith Certification Program"; a locksmith certification program administered by ILA
(acronym)

LLC
Limited Liability Company
(business)

PRP
abb. "Proficiency Registration Program"; a locksmith certification program administered by ALOA
(acronym)

RL
abb. The title "Registered Locksmith" as awarded by ALOA
(Certification)

RST
abb. the title "Registered Safe Technician" as awarded by NSO
(Certification)

STPRP
abb. "Safe Technicians Proficiency Registration Program"; the certification program of SAVTA as administered by ALOA
(acronym)

Abbreviations Related to Master Keying

A, AA, AA1, 1AA, etc.
key symbol - see also standard key coding system
(master keying)(keys)

ATT
abb. attendant's key
(master keying)

b-t
abb. bow-to-tip
(keys)(pinning)(cylinders and cores)(master keying)

BM
abb. block master key
(master keying)

BMK
abb. block master key
(master keying)

CBOK
abb. construction breakout key
(master keying)

CK
abb. change key
(master keying)(pinning)

CMK
abb. construction master key
(master keying)(pinning)

CMK'd
abb. construction master keyed
(master keying)(pinning)

CTK
abb. Control Key, used on pinning charts
(master keying)

CTRL
abb. control key
(master keying)

EMK
abb. emergency master key
(master keying)

ENG
abb. engineer's key
(master keying)

GGGMK
abb. great great grand master key
(master keying)

GGGMK'D
abb. great great grand master keyed
(master keying)((pinning)

GGM
abb. great grand master key
(master keying)

GGMK
abb. great grand master key
(master keying)

GGMK'D
abb. great grand master keyed
(master keying)(pinning)

GM
abb. grand master key
(master keying)

GMK
abb. grand master key
(master keying)

GMK section
abb. grand master key section
(master keying)

GMK'D
abb. grand master keyed
(master keying)(pinning)

HGM
abb. horizontal group master key
(master keying)

HKP
abb. housekeeper's key
(master keying)

HM
abb. Horizontal Master Key - see also HGM,HMK
(master keying)

HMK
abb. Horizontal Master Key – see also HGM,HM
(master keying)

IC
abb. interchangeable core
(master keying)(cylinders and cores)(pinning)

k
sym. symbol for "keys" used after a numerical designation of the quantity of the keys requested to be supplied with the cylinders; e.g., lk, 2k, 3k, etc. it is usually found in hardware/keying schedules.
(master keying)(keys)

KA
abb. keyed alike
(master keying)(pinning)

KA1, KA2, etc.
symbol which indicates that all cylinders so designated are or are to be operated by the same key(s). The numerical designation indicates the keyed alike group or set.
(master keying)(pinning)

KA/2, KA/3, etc.
symbol used to indicate the quantity of locks or cylinders in keyed alike groups. These groups are usually formed from a larger quantity; e.g., 30 cylinders KA/2.
(master keying)(pinning)(lock types)

KBA
abb. key bitting array
(master keying)

KD
abb. keyed different
(master keying)(pinning)

KWY
abb. keyway
(master keying)(keys)

LFIC
abb. Large Format Interchangeable Core
(master keying)(cylinders and cores)(pinning)

LPP
abb. Limited Position Progression
(master keying)

LM
abb. Line Master Key see also RM, Row Master Key
(master keying)

LRC
abb. Limited Rotating Constant
(master keying)

MACS
abb. maximum adjacent cut specification
(master keying)(key cutting)(keys)

MCCS
Abb. Maximum Compound Cut Specification
(master keying)(key cutting)(keys)

MK
abb. master key
(master keying)(keys)

MKCS
abb. modified key coding system
(master keying)

MK'd
abb. master keyed
(master keying)(cylinders and cores)(pinning)

MK'd only
abb. master keyed only
(master keying)(cylinders and cores)(pinning)

MK section
abb. master key section
(master keying)(cylinders and cores)(keys)

MOCS
abb. maximum opposing cut specification
(master keying)(cylinders and cores)(keys)

NCK
sym. symbol for "no change key," primarily used in hardware schedules
(master keying)(pinning)

NMK
abb. a notation used to indicate "not master keyed" and is suffixed in parentheses to a regular keying symbol. It indicates that the cylinder is not to be operated by the master key(s) specified in the regular keying symbol; e.g., AB6(NMK).
(master keying)(pinning)

NUR
abb. nurse's key
(master keying)

O.b.
abb. operated by, as used in keying schedules
(master keying)(pinning)

RCM
abb. Rotating Constant Method
(master keying)

RM
abb. row master key
(master keying)

SFIC
abb. Small Format Interchangeable Core
(master keying)(cylinders and cores)(pinning)(keys)

SKCS
abb. standard key coding system
(master keying)

SKD
sym. symbol for "single keyed", normally followed by a numerical designation in the standard key coding system; e.g., SKD1, SKD2, etc. It indicates that a cylinder or lock is not master keyed but is part of the keying system
(master keying)(pinning)

SMK
abb. sub-master key
(master keying)(keys)

SOP
abb. Sequence of Progression
(master keying)

t-b
abb. tip-to-bow
(keys)(pinning)(cylinders and cores)(master keying)

TMK
abb. top master key
(master keying)(pinning)

TPP
abb. Total Position Progression
(master keying)

VGM
abb. vertical group master key see also VM
(master keying)

VKC
abb. visual key control
(master keying)

VM
abb. vertical master key see also VGM
(master keying)

X
sym. symbol used in hardware schedules to indicate a cross-keyed condition for a particular cylinder; e.g., XAA2, XIX (but not AX7)
(master keying)(pinning)

Abbreviations related to Life Safety

ADA
abb. Americans with Disabilities Act
(acronym) (Life Safety)

AHJ
abb. authority having jurisdiction
(acronym) (Life Safety)

ANSI
abb. American National Standards Institute
(acronym)(Life Safety)

ASA
American Standards Association - See ANSI
(acronym)

CO
abb. certificate of occupancy
(Life Safety)

LH
abb. left hand
(basic safe work)(doors) (Life Safety)

LHR
abb. left hand reverse bevel
(doors)(Life Safety)

NRP
abb. non-removable pin
(hinges)(Life Safety)(doors)

RH
abb. right-hand
(basic safe work)(doors)(Life Safety)

RHR
abb. (right hand reverse bevel)
(doors)(Life Safety)

Abbreviations Related to Doors

LH
abb. left hand
(basic safe work)(doors)

LHR
abb. left hand reverse bevel
(doors)(Life Safety)

NRP
abb. non-removable pin
(hinges)(Life Safety)(doors)

RH
abb. right-hand
(basic safe work)(doors)(Life Safety)

RHR
abb. (right hand reverse bevel)
(doors)(Life Safety)

Abbreviations Related to Keys

A, AA, AA1, 1AA, etc.
key symbol - see also standard key coding system
(master keying)(keys)

b-t
abb. bow to tip
(keys)

k
sym. symbol for "keys" used after a numerical designation of the quantity of the keys requested to be supplied with the cylinders; e.g., lk, 2k, 3k, etc. it is usually found in hardware/keying schedules.
(master keying)(keys)

KWY
abb. keyway
(master keying)(keys)

MACS
abb. maximum adjacent cut specification
(master keying)(key cutting)(keys)

MCCS
Abb. Maximum Compound Cut Specification
(master keying)(key cutting)(keys)

MK
abb. master key
(master keying)(keys)

MK section
abb. master key section
(master keying)(cylinders and cores)(keys)

MOCS
abb. maximum opposing cut specification
(master keying)(cylinders and cores)(keys)

SFIC
abb. Small Format Interchangeable Core
(master keying)(cylinders and cores)(pinning)(keys)

SMK
abb. sub-master key
(master keying)(keys)

t-b
abb. tip-to-bow
(keys)(pinning)(cylinders and cores)(master keying)

Abbreviations Related to Pinning

CK
abb. change key
(master keying)(pinning)

CMK
abb. construction master key
(master keying)(pinning)

CMK'd
abb. construction master keyed
(master keying)(pinning)

CTK
abb. Control Key, used on pinning charts
(master keying)(pinning)

GGGMK'D
abb. great great grand master keyed
(master keying)((pinning)

GGMK'D
abb. great grand master keyed
(master keying)(pinning)

GMK'D
abb. grand master keyed
(master keying)(pinning)

IC
abb. interchangeable core
(master keying)(cylinders and cores)(pinning)

KA
abb. keyed alike
(master keying)(pinning)

KA1, KA2, etc.
symbol which indicates that all cylinders so designated are or are to be operated by the same key(s). The numerical designation indicates the keyed alike group or set.
(master keying)(pinning)

KA/2, KA/3, etc.
symbol used to indicate the quantity of locks or cylinders in keyed alike groups. These groups are usually formed from a larger quantity; e.g., 30 cylinders KA/2.
(master keying)(pinning)(lock types)

KD
abb. keyed different
(master keying)(pinning)

KR
abb. 1. keyed random 2. key retaining
(pinning)

LFIC
abb. Large Format Interchangeable Core
(master keying)(cylinders and cores)(pinning)

MK'd
abb. master keyed
(master keying)(cylinders and cores)(pinning)

MK'd only
abb. master keyed only
(master keying)(cylinders and cores)(pinning)

NCK
sym. symbol for "no change key," primarily used in hardware schedules
(master keying)(pinning)

NMK
abb. a notation used to indicate "not master keyed" and is suffixed in parentheses to a regular keying symbol. It indicates that the cylinder is not to be operated by the master key(s) specified in the regular keying symbol; e.g., AB6(NMK).
(master keying)(pinning)

O.b.
abb. operated by, as used in keying schedules
(master keying)(pinning)

SKD
sym. symbol for "single keyed", normally followed by a numerical designation in the standard key coding system; e.g., SKD1, SKD2, etc. It indicates that a cylinder or lock is not master keyed but is part of the keying system
(master keying)(pinning)

TMK
abb. top master key
(master keying)(pinning)

X
sym. symbol used in hardware schedules to indicate a cross-keyed condition for a particular cylinder; e.g., XAA2, XIX (but not AX7)
(master keying)(pinning)

Abbreviations related to Basic Safe Work

AED
abb. anti-explosive device
(basic safe work)

AHD
abb. after hours depository
(basic safe work)

ATM
abb. automatic teller machine
(basic safe work)

BCH
abb. bolt control handle
(basic safe work)

CCW
abb. Counter Clockwise, as used in combination dialing instructions
(basic safe work)

CW
abb. Clockwise, as used in combination dialing instructions
(basic safe work)

ERD
abb. external relocking device
(basic safe work)

HP
abb. hardplate
(basic safe work)

IRD
abb. internal relocking device
(basic safe work)

LH
abb. left hand
(basic safe work)(doors)

LHVD
abb. left hand vertical down
(basic safe work)

LHVU
abb. left hand vertical up
(basic safe work)

LOBC
abb. 1. locked on by combination, 2. (sic) locked on back cover
(basic safe work)

MP
abb. manipulation proof
(basic safe work)

MR
abb. manipulation resistant
(basic safe work)

RH
abb. right-hand
(basic safe work)(doors)(Life Safety)

RHVD
abb. right hand vertical down
(basic safe work)

RHVU
abb. right hand vertical up
(basic safe work)

RLD
abb. relocking device
(basic safe work)

RLT
abb. relock trigger
(basic safe work)

SDB
abb. safe deposit box
(basic safe work)

VD
abb. vertical down
(basic safe work)

VU
abb. vertical up
(basic safe work)

Abbreviations related to electronics, electromechanical, access control and computers

CAN
abb. controller area network
(electronics, electromechanical, access control and computers)

CICC
abb. contactless smart card
(electronics, electromechanical, access control and computers)

EAC
abb. electronic access control
(electronics, electromechanical, access control and computers)

ECM
abb. engine control module
(automotive)

FAR
abb. false acceptance rate
(electronics, electromechanical, access control and computers)

FRR
abb. false rejection rate
(electronics, electromechanical, access control and computers)

HiCo
abb. high coercivity
(electronics, electromechanical, access control and computers)

IP
abb. internet protocol
(electronics, electromechanical, access control and computers)

IR
abb. Infrared
(electronics, electromechanical, access control and computers)

LoCo
abb. low coercivity
(electronics, electromechanical, access control and computers)

NFS
abb. non-fail safe
(electronics, electromechanical, access control and computers)

Oe
abb. oersted
(electronics, electromechanical, access control and computers)

PATS
abb. Passive Anti-Theft System
(automotive) electronics, electromechanical, access control and computers)

PIN
abb. personal identification number
(electronics, electromechanical, access control and computers)

PIR
abb. passive infra-red
(electronics, electromechanical, access control and computers)

RF
abb. Radio Frequency
(electronics, electromechanical, access control and computers)

RFID
abb. radio frequency identification
(electronics, electromechanical, access control and computers)

TCP
abb. transmission control protocol
(electronics, electromechanical, access control and computers)

TCP/IP
n. the system networks use to communicate with one another
(electronics, electromechanical, access control and computers)

TTL
abb. 1. transistor to transistor logic, 2. time to live
(electronics, electromechanical, access control and computers)

VATS
abb. Vehicle Anti-Theft System
(automotive) (electronics, electromechanical, access control and computers)

Abbreviations related to electronics, electromechanical, access control and computers

CAN
abb. controller area network
(electronics, electromechanical, access control and computers)

CICC
abb. contactless smart card
(electronics, electromechanical, access control and computers)

EAC
abb. electronic access control
(electronics, electromechanical, access control and computers)

ECM
abb. engine control module
(automotive)

FAR
abb. false acceptance rate
(electronics, electromechanical, access control and computers)

FRR
abb. false rejection rate
(electronics, electromechanical, access control and computers)

HiCo
abb. high coercivity
(electronics, electromechanical, access control and computers)

IP
abb. internet protocol
(electronics, electromechanical, access control and computers)

IR
abb. Infrared
(electronics, electromechanical, access control and computers)

LoCo
abb. low coercivity
(electronics, electromechanical, access control and computers)

NFS
abb. non-fail safe
(electronics, electromechanical, access control and computers)

Oe
abb. oersted
(electronics, electromechanical, access control and computers)

PATS
abb. Passive Anti-Theft System
(automotive) electronics, electromechanical, access control and computers)

PIN
abb. personal identification number
(electronics, electromechanical, access control and computers)

PIR
abb. passive infra-red
(electronics, electromechanical, access control and computers)

RF
abb. Radio Frequency
(electronics, electromechanical, access control and computers)

RFID
abb. radio frequency identification
(electronics, electromechanical, access control and computers)

TCP
abb. transmission control protocol
(electronics, electromechanical, access control and computers)

TCP/IP
n. the system networks use to communicate with one another
(electronics, electromechanical, access control and computers)

TTL
abb. 1. transistor to transistor logic, 2. time to live
(electronics, electromechanical, access control and computers)

VATS
abb. Vehicle Anti-Theft System
(automotive) (electronics, electromechanical, access control and computers)

Abbreviations Related to Utility Locks

KR
abb. 1. keyed random 2. key retaining
(pinning)

NKR
abb. non key retaining
(utility locks)

NRK
abb. non-removable key
(utility locks)

Abbreviations Related to Hinges

NRP
abb. non-removable pin
(hinges)(Life Safety)(doors)

TBB
abb. template ball bearing
(hinges)(Life Safety)

Abbreviations Related to Lock Types

KIK
abb. Key-in-Knob
(lock types)

KIL
abb. Key-in-Lever
(lock types)

Section Thirteen: Electives for CJIL and CMIL

When it comes to the elective portion of the certification, either you are familiar with a product or you are not. It is not as simple as merely defining terms. Nonetheless, you should know where to go to become aware of the product. The purpose of this book is NOT to teach you locksmithing, and certainly not a specific brand of locks. It is to prepare you for an exam on the topic. The manufacturers or educators have entire volumes on each elective. It is not our goal to duplicate their efforts or take away from them. What we will attempt to do here is guide you as to the areas the exams focus on and the quickest documentation we can locate to allow you to review it.

Electives E1, E2 & E3 – Small Format Interchangeable Core Systems
A2, A3 & A4 (BEST Style)

The first thing to keep in mind is that the cores and keys are all the same for A2., A3 and A4; only the pinning segments change. Some of the service equipment will change depending on the keying system used. The method of pinning cores is the same except for the math used to create the stack heights. You will have a bottom pin (A, C, E) pin, a master pin if the core is mastered (B, D, F), a buildup pin (B, D, F) and a driver pin (B, D, F) in each chamber.

	A2	A3	A4
Stack Height	23	16	14
Build up	10	7	6
Segments	0-9	0-6	0-5
Bottom Pin	A	C	E
Master, Build up, Driver	B	D	F
Increments size	0.0125	0.018	0.021

Reference material:

SFIC and MFIC Interchangeable Core Servicing
by Don OShall #ILA_SFIC
http://store.ILA-resources.com
or
http://www.institutionallocksmiths.org/store/book1-1.htm

Schlage SFIC Service Manual
covers the A2 system but is also useful for A3 and A4. The most recent version can be downloaded from the Schlage website. However, theree is no direct link
provided on the site, so you have to use a search engine like Google or Yahoo. It is part # SC5292 Rev. 12/07

Most direct link at time of publication:
http://us.allegion.com/IRSTDocs/Catalog/109487.pdf
or
http://us.allegion.com/Products/mechanical_locks/service_support/literature/Pages/default.aspx

KeyMark Technical Manual
available from a few of the ASSA/ABLOY companies like Yale and Medeco. The Yale version is available on their website http://www.yalecommercial.com under the "product information & documentation" tab then "parts service manuals." The Medeco version can be obtained from any Medeco representative.
Most direct link to Yale version at time of publication:
http://extranet.assabloydss.com/library/partsmanuals/Yale/pdf/422SO.pdf

Recommended reading:
Don OShall Guide to Interchangeable Core Servicing
by Don OShall # ILA-DO12IC
http://store.ILA-resources.com
or
http://www.institutionallocksmiths.org/store/book1-1.htm

How to pin and service an SFIC core eBook
mini-book by Don OShall
http://www.locksmithingeducation.com/catalog.htm

*Core of the Matter**
by A.J. Hoffman and Billy B. Edwards, Jr
http://www.Locksoft.com

The National Locksmith Guide to Interchangeable Core Cylinders
by Don O'Shall
The National Locksmith (Ccurrently out of print.)
(Available on Amazon.com and at KeylessLocks.com)

The National Locksmith Interchangeable Cores Small Format
By William M. Lynk
The National Locksmith bookstore

Small Format and Mixed Format Interchangeable Cores
by Don OShall
http://www.eBay.com

ELECTIVE E4
HISTORY

History is vital to any industry! You should visit the **Lock Museum of America**- online or in person, if you get a chance to. It is located in Terryville, Connecticut..

Recommended reading:

Locks and Locksmiths of America
Thomas Hennessy
Locksmith Publishing Co.

The Builders Hardware Industry
Walter McAninch
The Ballard Locks Publishing Co.

The Complete Book of Locks and Locksmithing
Bill Phillips
McGraw-Hill

The Lure of the Lock
General Society of Mechanics and Tradesmen of the City of New York building, 20 West 44th Street (midtown Manhattan), NYC,NY

Also available on Amazon:
http://www.amazon.com/

Early Locks and Lockmakers in America
by Thomas Hennessy
Nickerson & Collins Pub. Co., Locksmith Ledger Division (1976)

Also available on Amazon
http://www.amazon.com/

Elective E5 - Life Safety

This exam covers building and fire codes primarily, with a strong emphasis on NFPA 80 and NFPA 101.

Recommended reading:

IR Fire Life and Safety Code Book
Schlage (Division of Allegion - formerly Ingersoll-Rand)
available as free download at:
ILA Bookstore
http://www.institutionallocksmiths.org/store/book2-1.htm

Life Safety Codes with UL and ADA
by Tom Demont
Available from the ALOA bookstore or direct from author
http://www.aloa.org

International Building Code
International Code Council
http://www.iccsafe.org/
Free online version:
http://publiccodes.cyberregs.com/icod/ibc/index.htm

NFPA 101 Life Safety Code
National Fire Protection Association
http://www.nfpa.org/codes-and-standards/document-information-pages?mode=code&code=101

(with optional free access online with online registration)

or

http://www.nfpa.org/catalog/product.asp?pid=10112&order_src=A383&gclid=CIHAtJKH5b0CFa_m7AodWUEAfg&cookie_test=1

Elective E6 –
Corbin Russwin Cylinder Servicing

This test concentrates more on Corbin than Russwin, and knowledge of the numbering systems for X and Z series in both pre-1970 and System 70 patterns is essential. Questions include Corbin original part numbers for pins and springs and some basic general key troubleshooting.

The single best reference manual for this elective is the book *Corbin Russwin Cylinder Manual.*

At of the time of publication the most recent version was available for download from the Corbin Russwin website:
http://www.corbinrusswin.com
under the "parts/service manuals" tab. A printed copy may still be available also from your local ASSA ABLOY DSS representative.

Recommended reading:

Most direct link at time of publication:
http://extranet.assaabloydss.com/library/partsmanuals/CorbinRusswin/pdf/
CR CylinderManual.pdf

Much of the original version of the *Corbin Russwin Cylinder Manual* was written by A.J. Hoffman. Another book primarily written by A.J. that covers some of the Corbin Russwin products is *Core of the Matter** by A.J. Hoffman and Bill Edwards.
Available from some lock suppliers or direct from the publisher,
Locksoft.com at:

http://www.thelockman.com/publish/buynow.htm

ILA has made arrangements with Corbin-Russwin to provide the cylinder manual as a free download through their ILA Bookstore at:

http://store.ila-resources.com/book2-1.htm

or

http://www.institutionallocksmiths.org/store/book2-1.htm

Elective E7 – Medeco

Medeco has some of the best support and training material of all the lock manufacturers. The elective was developed with the outstanding support of Medeco staff. All the information you need is covered in Medeco's certified classes and their technical manuals. Medeco manuals are not generally available for download but can be ordered from them, or contact your local Medeco representative. Some useful information to know is that Medeco products which involve angle cuts, such as Classic Commercial Medeco and Biaxial versions, identify the angles with the bittings using a series of letters. These can be confusing to look at if you do not understand how they were developed. The original letters were L, C and R for Left, Center and Right. Biaxial and later products use 'fore' and 'aft' angles. The 'fore' angles use the letters BEFORE L, C and R - in other words, K, B and Q. The 'Aft' angles use the letters AFTER L, C and R, - M, D and S.

Recommended reading:

KeyMark Technical Manual
Part# LT-807028

Keymark X4 brochure
Part # LT 922123

Tech Service Manual Original & Biaxial
Part # LT-807029

Biaxial Medeco3 Tech Manual
Part # LT-922088 Rev B

Medeco Technical Manual
free download by special arrangement at:
http://store.ila-resources.com/book2-1.htm
or
http://www.institutionallocksmiths.org/store/book2-1.htm

Elective E8
BEST Hardware Servicing

This elective covers BEST door hardware only, not their key systems.

Much of the test consists of recognizing the functions associated with the Letter in the product number, such as L for Privacy Latch function, 0 for Passage, A for Entry/corridor, D for Storeroom, R for Classroom, etc. and recognizing the difference between Grade one numbering and Grade 2 numbering, including the 2 for -3/8 backset and 3 for 2 and three quarters inch backset.

Their primary literature page at the time of publication is:

https://support.stanleysecurity.com/hc/en-us/categories/200102876-BEST-ACCESS-SYSTEMS

Some brochures and manuals are available through special arrangement with them from:

http://store.ila-resoures.com/book2-1.htm

or

http://www.institutionallocksmiths.org/store/book2-1.htm

Elective E9 –
Corbin Russwin Door Hardware

Much of this test still refers to pinning, particularly of the large format interchangeable core product and master ring product. The remainder of the questions range from knowledge of functions and part numbers identifying common functions, and some basic trouble-shooting and servicing. You should be knowledgeable on the difference between servicing -old-stylell and -newer stylell knobs, and you should know how to tell when a key has been cut too deep or too shallow.

The best study materials for this elective are their full catalog and the parts catalog.

http://www.corbinrusswin.com.

The cylinder service manual can help understand some of the product line options and is available as a free download in many places, including the Corbin-Russwin web site and the ILA Bookstore.

Corbin-Russwin Cylinder Servicing Manual
http://store.ila-resources.com/book2-1.htm
or
http://www.institutionallocksmiths.org/store/book2-1.htm

ELECTIVE E10
Schlage Everest

Classic Schlage Everest is a lower cost alternative to Patented Key Control. It has three series, identified by the letters B, C and D.

The B series is a small format core, which uses traditional Small Format core pinning in a patented key product., which uses a check pin to achieve the patent protection. Its keyways are not compatible with Primus products.

The C and D are full size cylinders and cores with a check pin. Their keyways can be compatible with Primus keyways. The difference between C and D is that D is restricted to specific customers in each area, whereas C is an open license sold through locksmith distribution channels.

Recommended Reading:

Everest Full Size Cylinder Manual
http://us.allegion.com/Products/mechanical_locks/service_support/literature/Pages/default.aspx

Available as a free download by special arrangement from:
http://store.ila-resources.com/book2-1.htm
or
http://www.institutionallocksmiths.org/store/book2-1.htm

Schlage Key Systems Cylinders and Keys Reference Guide
http://us.allegion.com/IRSTDocs/Catalog/109487.pdf
Available as a free download by special arrangement from:
http://store.ila-resources.com/book2-1.htm
or
http://www.institutionallocksmiths.org/store/book2-1.htm

Cylinders and Key Blanks Quick Reference Guide
http://us.allegion.com/IRSTDocs/Catalog/109158.pdf
Available as a free download by special arrangement from:
http://store.ila-resources.com/book2-1.htm
or
http://www.institutionallocksmiths.org/store/book2-1.htm

Elective E11 Classic KABA Peaks

Classic KABA Peaks offers many SFIC, MFIC and LFIC options as well as full size cylinders. The parts manual is one of the best sources of information regarding servicing these cylinders and cores.

Recommended reading:

The Journeyman Guide to servicing Classic Kaba Peaks
by Don OShall
http://www.LocksmithingEducation.com/catalog.htm

Recommended reading:

http://www.kaba-ilco.com/key-systems/literature-support/literature/624686/key-control-cylinders.html

http://www.kaba-ilco.com/key-systems/products/key-control-cylinders/630162/peaks-classic.html

Peaks Classic Preferred Technical Manual
Available as a free download by special arrangement from:
http://store.ila-resources.com/book2-1.htm
or
http://www.institutionallocksmiths.org/store/book2-1.htm

KABA_Parts_Book_Peaks_Classic
Available as a free download by special arrangement from:
http://store.ila-resources.com/book2-1.htm
or
http://www.institutionallocksmiths.org/store/book2-1.htm

The following will help with future exams related to KABA cylinders and keying:

Peaks Global Technical Manual
Available as a free download by special arrangement from:
http://store.ila-resources.com/book2-1.htm
or
http://www.institutionallocksmiths.org/store/book2-1.htm

Peaks Global_Parts_Book
Available as a free download by special arrangement from:
http://store.ila-resources.com/book2-1.htm
or
http://www.institutionallocksmiths.org/store/book2-1.htm

Peaks Preferred Parts Book
Available as a free download by special arrangement from:
http://store.ila-resources.com/book2-1.htm
or
http://www.institutionallocksmiths.org/store/book2-1.htm

Elective E12 - Master Keying, Basic

There are many places that you can get basic master keying classes and sources. All the major lock manufactures' websites will reference master keying or even list material for laying out a s system. The problem is almost none of them have material for how to create
a s system. They are all designed to teach you how to define a s system in order to have them
build the master key system for you.

Realistically, the only ways to learn master keying is to take a class or read books. Master keying classes are offered by many manufactures in varying degree of quality depending on how much the company embraces customers using non-factory designed systems. Other than manufactures, some distributors and many associations - both local and national - sponsor master keying classes.

There are many informative books available that will give you a basic foundation, and then some. Below I have just listed a few that I have found helpful, and know they contain the information covered in the elective.

Most of what is necessary for the E12 exam is found in the terminology section of this Study Guide.

Recommended reading:

Master Keying Textbook-
by Don O'Shall and Tony West Locksmithing
Education publishing
http://www.locksmithingEducation.com/catalog.htm
(also available at ILA Bookstore)
http://store.ila-resources.com
or
http://www.institutionallocksmiths.org/store/book1-1.htm

Master Keying by the Numbers by Billy B.
Edwards, Jr.
http://www.thelockman.com/publish/buynow.htm

Basic Master Keying - QBE
by Don O'Shall and John Truempy
Locksmithing Education publishing
http://www.locksmithingEducation.com/catalog.htm (also available at ILA Bookstore)
http://store.ila-resources.com
or
http://www.institutionallocksmiths.org/store/book1-1.htm

Advanced Master Keying Skills
by Don O'Shall and John Truempy
Locksmithing Education publishing
http://www.locksmithingEducation.com/catalog.htm
(also available at ILA Bookstore)
http://store.ila-resources.com
or
http://www.institutionallocksmiths.org/store/book1-1.htm

Fundamentals of Master Keying: An Introduction to Split Pin Master Keying
by Jerome V. Andrews
Available from ALOA book store

Elective E13 – Von Duprin

Von Duprin has a few different panic bars in their product line: 99, 88, 33 etc. Each product also had different applications: rim mounted, mortise lock, and vertical rods both concealed and surface mounted.

The test was designed around the knowledge of the different products and their various applications. You will get the most information from catalogs, part catalogs and application guides from the company's web site:

http://www.vonduprin.com

You can also get copies of the catalogs and other material from your local Ingersoll Rand representative or by contacting their customer service department at:

Von Duprin
2720 Tobey Dr
Indianapolis, IN 46219

Elective E14 – Rixson

Most of the information needed for this test can be found in their product catalogs and end user information literature available on the Rixson web site: There are essentially three product lines covered: in-floor closers, overhead closers and pivots.
Most of the questions deal with the in-floor models, for which Rison is best known. The user's guide on their webpage can be very informative.

http://www.rixson.com/

Elective E15 – Kwikset

This elective covers both cylinder servicing and the Kwikset product line, but STRICTLY the pin tumbler products, not their 'Smart' products. Their 'Smart' products generally do not meet the needs of institutions.. It's important to study both the Kwikset catalog and the rekeying manual listed below.

Recommended reading:

Kwikset Pin Tumbler & Cylinder Service Manual
Courtesy of Kwikset Lock
http://www.ila-resources.com/store/book2-1.htm
or
http://www.institutionallocksmiths.org/store/book2-1.htm

Kwikset 2004 Rekeying Manual.
Part # LIT 7-2-0112/03

Available from the Kwikset website www.kwikset.com under the "trade resources" tab. It is also be available from your Kwikset representative.

Elective E16 – Primus

Schlage Primus is strictly a full size cylinder and core product - no SFIC. It is patent protected with the original patent expiring in 2014 and the new model in 2027. The features which offer key control are the undercut groove, and the five finger pins. It is available in both C and D series patent protected keyways, and some are compatible with C and D series Everest.

Recommended reading:

http://us.allegion.com/Products/mechanical_locks/service_support/literature/Pages/default.aspx

Primus Service Manual
http://us.allegion.com/IRSTDocs/Manual/108482.pdf
also available as a free download at:
http://www.ila-resources.com/store/book2-1.htm
or
http://www.institutionallocksmiths.org/store/book2-1.htm
Courtesy of Schlage Lock

Everest Primus Full Size Cylinder Manual
http://www.kleineandsons.com/detailed/schlage/pdf/key/MS-C80_Everest_Srvc_Man.pdf

Elective E17 – Schlage Large Format and Full Size

This test is for all of Schlage's other keying systems not considered restricted or high security. Most of the information can be found in product line catalogs and service manuals. The Schlage web site (http://www.schlage.com) is divided into two parts: consumer products and commercial products. Both sections contain information that can be useful for this test.

Recommended reading :

Schlage Cylinders, Keys and Key Control
Courtesy of Schlage Lock
http://www.ila-resources.com/store/book2-1.htm

http://www.consumer.schlage.com/Project%2oDocuments/Psi3-325.pdf

http://professional.schlage.com/literature/literature.asp

Elective E18 – ASSA Twin 6000, Twin Exclusive, Twin V-10 & Twin Pro

ASSA is similar to Medeco in that not all of their service information is available online but some general information can be found there. The ASSA web site is:
http://www.assalock.com

a more direct link to their literature is:
http://www.assalock.com/download.htm

Another great source for this information is your ASSA lock representative. Many of them have participated in the ILCP and will be more than happy to provide the information you need.

Recommended Reading:

ASSA Technical Manual
Courtesy of ASSA, USA
http://www.ila-resources.com/store/book2-1.htm
or
http://www.institutionallocksmiths.org/store/book2-1.htm

Investigative Locksmith Techniques

(Elective number unassigned at press time.)

Investigative locksmithing is a growing field of expertise in the industry. Knowledge in this field is beneficial to the institutional locksmith with regard to conducting investigations into breaches of security and crime scenes. It's also valuable when performing security surveys.

The most valuable aid in studying for this exam are the Investigative Locksmith I, II
& III classes sponsored at various times throughout the year by the International
Association of Investigative Locksmiths (IAIL).

Recommended reading:

IAIL Journal, March 2002

IAIL Journal, May 2003

IAIL Forensic Locksmith Manual
International Association of Investigative Locksmiths

Pocket Partner
by D. Evers, M. Miller, T. Glover
Sequoia

Recommended industry classes:

Investigative Locksmithing, Levels 1, 2 & 3 (IAIL)

Forensic Photography for the Investigative Locksmith (IAIL)

Electronic Access Control Theory
(Elective number unassigned at press time.)

This exam concentrates on concepts and theories of electronic access control (EAC). It generally does not address field installation or troubleshooting techniques.

Since there isn't a definitive resource for EAC terms, many different resources were consulted for definitions. Whenever possible, priority was given to the definition found in the LIST Council Dictionary. Still, not every term used in this exam is so precisely defined as to be easily found in any of the listed resources, and definitions for the same term vary wildly among the resources listed below.

Recommended reading:

NFPA Pocket Guide to Electronic Security System Installation
by Shane M. Clary
NFPA

The ADI Access Control Glossary of Terms
http://w6.adi-dist.com/shared/library/docLibrazy.aspx?f=5

ASIS International Glossary of Security Terms
www.asisonline.org/library/glossary/index.xml

The GE Security Glossary
http://www.gesecurity.com/portal/site/GESecurity/menuitem.dcz6gS440e230209942dsze714004tca/?vgnextoid=682at48067b330IOVgnVCMtoooo0410014acRCRD

Recommended industry classes:

Access Control
(ALOA)

Basic of Alarms and Card Access
(DOS Educational Services,
a division of Lounging Lizard Publishing)
taught by Tony West

Note: Because manufacturers frequently change web page names and links, wherever they could get permission to do so, links to a free download through the ILA or through Locksmithing Education, LLC have been provided.

All free links are to the original manufacturer's manual and are not owned, printed or supported by the ILA or Locksmithing Education, LLC.

If the manufacturer decides they no longer wish them to provide the download availability they will be removed and neither the ILA nor LocksmithingEducation.com should be expected to provide an alternative.

All links shown are current as of the time of initial publication of this guide.